WINNING
THE PROFESSIONAL
SERVICES
SALE

WINNING
THE PROFESSIONAL
SERVICES
SALE

Unconventional Strategies to
Reach More Clients, Land
Profitable Work, and Maintain
Your Sanity

MICHAEL W. McLAUGHLIN

WILEY

John Wiley & Sons, Inc.

Published by John Wiley & Sons, Inc., Hoboken, New Jersey.

Published simultaneously in Canada.

For general information on our other products and services or for technical support, please contact our Customer Care Department within the United States at (800) 762-2974, outside the United States at (317) 572-3993, or fax (317) 572-4002.

Wiley also publishes its books in a variety of electronic formats. Some content that appears in print may not be available in electronic books. For more information about Wiley products, visit our web site at www.wiley.com.

Library of Congress Cataloging-in-Publication Data:

McLaughlin, Michael W., 1955-
Winning the professional services sale : unconventional strategies to reach more clients, land profitable work, and maintain your sanity / by Michael W. McLaughlin.
     p. cm.
  Includes bibliographical references and index.
  ISBN 978-0-470-45585-2 (cloth)
  1. Selling. 2. Success in business. I. Title.
  HF5438.25.M399 2009
  658.85–dc22   2009008844

Printed in the United States of America
10 9 8 7 6 5 4 3 2 1

For Sally

CONTENTS

ACKNOWLEDGMENTS

It wasn't my initial intent to write the book you're holding in your hands. At the outset, I had a different idea. But my agent, David Fugate, tested the market and helped me broaden the concept for the project. And he did that with patience, perseverance, and publishing industry expertise that is second to none. Thanks, David—without your help, this book wouldn't have made it to the market.

So many people influenced my thinking and lent a hand with this project that I risk leaving someone out unintentionally. But special thanks to my friends and colleagues, Fiona Czerniawska, Jeffrey Fox, Seth Godin, Ford Harding, Tom Sant, and Andrew Sobel.

I'm also grateful to Jay Conrad Levinson, the father of Guerrilla Marketing, and the coauthor of my first book, *Guerrilla Marketing for Consultants*. Thanks, Jay, for helping me understand the art and the business of writing a book.

Many of the perspectives in this book were forged by my experiences with the clients I've served over the years—both those who said yes to my proposals and the ones that got away. Just about everything I know about selling services came from those clients. I am indebted to each and every one of them and I've tried to reflect their voices and their lessons in these pages.

And, as importantly, the book distills what I've learned from the thousands of professionals I've met and worked with since the publication of my previous book. Thanks to all of you who told me what works for you and what doesn't. This book is enriched by your collective wisdom.

The team at John Wiley & Sons, Inc., makes the hard work of publishing feel easy. My editor, Shannon Vargo, always knew exactly what to do and when to do it. Beth Zipko never missed an editorial detail, nor did she leave any question unanswered. The sales, production, and marketing teams, who work so hard to convert a manuscript into a book, may not know how easy they are to work with. For their efforts, I am entirely grateful.

No matter how well you manage your time, writing a book becomes a big part of your life—and your family's life too. My wife, Sally, pushed this book along from a single idea to a completed manuscript. I can't count the hours she spent sharpening the ideas, editing the text, and preparing the manuscript for publication. If it wasn't for her, the book just wouldn't have gotten done. From the first time we met, I knew I was a lucky man. I wish everyone could experience such joy.

"You're gonna need a bigger boat."[1]

You might recognize that line from the movie, *Jaws*, in which a great white shark terrorizes beachgoers at the seaside community of Amity Island. While out in the newly hired shark hunter's boat, the town's police chief takes in the enormity of the beast up close and utters that now-famous understatement.

When facing extraordinary challenges, we often find our existing remedies inadequate. So we use all our resources and best ideas until we figure out how to overcome the latest obstacles. In other words, we find a bigger boat.

If there ever was a time when professional services sellers needed new strategies and tools (a bigger, *better* boat), this is it. In the not-too-distant past, you *knew* what to do. Before you met a client for the first time, you would run through a familiar checklist of everything you needed to consider. You would think through your service offering and brush up on your rapport builders. Then you would listen to what the client wanted, offer a solution, handle objections, and close the sale. For the most part, that approach used to work. But some not-so-subtle changes have crept into the services sales process, short-circuiting the power of this routine approach.

For starters, clients began asking tougher questions and demanding more precise answers, including exactly how sellers would deliver their services and who would do the work. No longer satisfied with resumes to make their assessments, clients insisted on handpicking the people they wanted. In some cases, buyers asked sellers to create working prototypes of their proposed solution, offer previously completed work product as examples, and participate in mock workshops to demonstrate that they really knew what they were doing.

Complicating matters, the client might hand over the purchase of the service to a procurement manager for negotiation, creating a buffer between the seller and the real buyer. Procurement executives, always anxious to cut the best deals possible, tend to emphasize price, terms, and conditions instead of the substance of proposals.

Clients have become impatient with the passive role of sitting back and waiting for a sales proposal from the supposed expert, instead demanding a hand in the process from the beginning. And they insist that services providers customize proposals and presentations down to the last detail. Generic claims from sellers, such as "Clients are our first priority," have ended up as roadkill on the highway to success.

In short, clients have grown weary of constantly keeping their guard up against false sincerity, artificial deadlines, and programmed strategies that salespeople were trained to use. If you need evidence of this fact, just reflect on how hard it can be to get an appointment with anyone other than an intermediary, even if you have something a client needs. If you ask 20 prospective buyers if they'd rather spend the afternoon with a dentist or a salesperson, most will dash to the dentist's chair.

Sales executives did hear these messages from buyers and responded with what some salespeople still call "customer-focused" sales strategies. Supposedly, these put the client's interests, not the seller's desire for a commission, at the center of the sales process. But, to many clients, these strategies looked like the same old seller-centric ones in a new guise.

The predictable outcome is that the client's perspective about service providers has shifted from "We trust you" to "Prove it." This is understandable. After years of listening to sales pitches, clients realize that relying solely on sellers' promises is no longer enough to arrive at a decision. They want more certainty about potential results and risks before they commit their resources. Asking for proof of sellers' assertions is a logical place to start. What clients are really saying is that they want another way to buy services.

For sellers, this transformation means that the services sale has taken on all the characteristics of a complex project, not just a sales pitch. The salesperson, in effect, has become a project manager—solving clients' real problems, persuasively advocating for change, and managing the complex sales process. Salespeople are discovering that they not only have to develop superb selling skills, but competence in consultative abilities such as problem analysis, solution development, project management, and change management, to name a few.

Why Services Selling Must Change

One problem for services sellers who try to respond to these buyer demands is the outmoded definition of *selling,* which has its roots in the history of the product sale. For a business that sells bookcases, the buyer's need is clear—a place for storing books. What drives that sale is the features, benefits, and price of the bookcases. But if clients are struggling with how to improve employee retention, cut shipping costs, or accelerate business growth, for example, what clients say they want may not be what they really need.

And, unlike those selling products, services sellers can't afford to sit back in a showroom, waiting for a buyer to arrive with a ready-made need and a credit card. Today's services seller must be active in the market, offering ideas and solutions that *generate* client demand, and then they must be able to put together a winning sales strategy to satisfy that demand. What sets service providers apart from other sellers is that they are first and foremost *idea merchants.*

Before they can sell anything, they must sway clients with their ideas for change. Only then can they attempt to sell their services. This is where traditional sales advice falls short. Without recognition of their role as purveyors of ideas, sellers get trapped in common mistakes, such as trying to close the sale prematurely or preparing sales proposals before the client's problem is certain. As a result, if they win the sale at all, sometimes they solve the real problem; but it's equally possible that they end up treating symptoms and nothing really changes for their clients.

What Is a Professional Service?

A professional service is the performance of tasks designed to address a client's business issue(s) or need(s)—for a fee. A services sale is most often an individualized offering, such as an advertising campaign or a new business strategy. It usually requires more than a single sales call to close and, often, an extended time to deliver.

If you sell or deliver professional services, you know how much one client's buying process can differ from another's. You could find that one client wants a traditional dog and pony show for the sales presentation. Another client may want to see a prototype of your solution. Sometimes, clients want the process to have the precision of a symphony; other situations call for improvisation. Your sales process must accommodate either approach, or both. Instead of just listening to what you have to say, today's clients may dictate the buying process, or at least they're likely to want a hand in designing it.

But the client's participation in the sales process doesn't stop there. Today's clients often want to coinvent the solutions to their problem with you during the sales process. More and more, clients insist on defining, along with you, every aspect of the service. It is less common for clients to agree to iron out unresolved issues during the delivery of the service. This means that clients are stepping up to take ownership of the solutions they create with you.

These trends, the buyer-designed sales process, coinvention of services, and client ownership of the solution, impact every aspect of the services sale. If nothing else, these trends should tell you that you need new rules for selling professional services. More flexible strategies and tactics will leave the cookie-cutter sales processes in the dust. The intention of this book is to help you reach more clients and win profitable work—without losing your sanity.

The New Environment for Selling Services	
Then	**Now**
Sellers	Idea merchants
Help us	Show us
Offer a service	Coinvent a solution
Sell	Facilitate buying
Manage the sale	Manage change
Qualifications	Results
Few decision makers	Distributed decision making
Good work	What else can you do?
Assert credentials	Prove value
Sales techniques	Tell a story

What You'll Get

Whether your company sells business services, legal advice, outsourcing solutions, or management consulting, this book is for you. And, if you offer a professional service that is bundled with a product (or sold separately), you, too, will benefit from the concepts outlined here. In these pages, you'll find strategies and tools for winning the complex services sale, whether you are a sales force of one or part of a team. You won't find a monolithic sales process, but a set of consultative sales tools to help you identify the right opportunities and land the most profitable work—no matter what services you sell or who you sell them to. For those of you who already have a sales methodology, the principles in this book offer a powerful addition to your preexisting sales process.

Three essential concepts are the backbone of this book: First, in today's market every sales situation, whatever its size, evolves in predictable ways, and your approach to pursuing the sale must be mindful of this fact. Second, you may offer the same services to every client, but the way those clients buy and the issues you must address will be different every time. That means you must build a winning sales approach dynamically, as each sale unfolds. And finally, the professional services sale is a consultative process, which demands that sellers develop a broader perspective on the client's business than the sale right in front of them.

To help you respond to these realities and buying trends, the book offers a multipart framework, called "The Three Cs of Winning the Professional Services Sale: Connect, Collaborate, and Commit." This framework is *not* a rigid, linear progression of sales activities, but a way to organize a client-specific strategy that leads to a profitable sale.

The Three Cs framework stresses that the professional services sale is a consultative endeavor in which the seller, in collaboration with the client, uses the tools of the business adviser to understand the real issue facing the client. Then, with a clear view of the challenge, the seller and buyer coinvent a range of solutions that reflect the choices the client can make to address the issue. You differentiate those choices by factors such as expected value, complexity to implement, risk, and cost.

Part 1, "Connect," which helps you launch the sales process, begins with a rundown on the competitive realities confronting services sellers. Then I'll show you how to get off to a fast start with every sales opportunity through targeted preparation, efficient data collection, and insightful analysis of the client's issue. The emphasis throughout Connect is on the need to establish your unquestioned competence as the foundation for productive client relationships.

The Three Cs of Winning the Professional Services Sale

Connect	Collaborate	Commit
Prepare Efficiently	Know When to Walk Away	Make the Case for Change
Interview Clients with Insight	Craft Your Story	Guide the Sale to Closure
	Understand Buyer Motivations	Learn What Worked and What Didn't
Uncover the Real Problem	Anticipate Shifts	Cultivate Your Client Network
	Compel with Your Proposal	

Become Clients' Go-to Resource

Part 2, "Collaborate," lays out how to guide the client from the definition of the problem to a workable sales proposal, if that's the direction you and the buyer agree on. The underlying idea here is that your eventual profit—and your level of stress—are often determined during this stage of the sale. This part of the Three Cs provides a systematic way to make the (sometimes) tough decision to pursue an opportunity or leave it for someone else. It also offers advice on understanding buyers' motivations, crafting a winning sales strategy, managing inevitable surprises that crop up during the sales process, and designing the perfect sales proposal.

Among other things, Part 3, "Commit," shows you how to tell the story about clients' issues in a way that leads them to buy from you. Given the complexity of professional services offers, many sellers also assume the role of negotiator. If that's you, then you'll be able to use the advice on how to close a profitable sale while strengthening the client relationship.

No matter whether you win or lose a sale, you should use the wealth of intelligence you gain from the experience to refine your subsequent attempts to sell. To that end, the section about Commit also includes a way to look back at the sales process with clients to learn what worked and what didn't. This part of the framework also covers how to kick off your client projects and cultivate your network of client relationships. You'll find tips for building resilient client relationships that will support you on your current project and on future ones, too.

The Three Cs framework shows you how to become the go-to resource for clients, which should be your goal. You'll be the first one who comes to mind when your clients need help because of the strength of your ideas and the depth of your relationships.

The final section of the book, "Challenges," offers a practical guide for becoming a top-performing seller. The concept here, which I call the Seven by Seven Seller, outlines the roles and skills you must master to consistently land the work you really want.

And if you're a sales manager or executive, look for advice on how to identify potential sellers with just the right mix of talent and skills to become your next rainmaker. You'll also find suggestions for customizing professional development programs to cultivate the traits you want in all your salespeople.

Throughout the book, dozens of sidebars offer tips to make every part of the sales process more positive for your buyers and more productive for you. I've also included "Sanity Checks" along the way to suggest ideas for easing the pressures of selling and to challenge conventional assumptions about how to win the professional services sale.

The examples and stories in the book illustrate why some things work and others do not. These are based on real experiences, but I've changed the names and other details about the people involved to protect their confidences.

For simplicity, I use the term *client* or *buyer* throughout the book to mean either prospective or existing customer or client. I also use the terms *seller* and *salesperson* interchangeably to indicate the individual(s) working on the sales opportunity, whether they are business development professionals or service providers who have responsibility to both sell *and* deliver their services.

Those who offer professional services to clients are a diverse group, and each type of provider has its own terminology and jargon. Some of you may refer to your work with clients as *cases, engagements, initiatives,* or *projects,* and I use these terms interchangeably.

Just to be clear, this isn't a theoretical book on sales. For more than two decades, I've sold and delivered professional services, from one-week assessments handled by a single person to multiyear initiatives staffed by hundreds of people—and everything in between. Most of those sales were purely for services; but some were bundled sales, meaning they included a product and service component. I do not attempt to offer advice on selling products exclusively. Most books that attempt to straddle the worlds of selling products *and* services end up treating neither subject with the care it deserves.

Whether your title is business development executive, account manager, salesperson, consultant, or sales manager, you will find something of value in this book. The successful salesperson, both now and in the future, will be a consultant, project manager, problem solver, change agent, and seller all rolled into one. You'll consistently win the professional services sale if you approach each opportunity with two ideas in mind. First, your interests and those of your clients are inseparable. Your challenge is to help clients see that you genuinely believe that. Second, top sellers consistently land the most profitable work by realizing that drawing clients to them through the power of ideas is far more effective than chasing buyers with outmoded sales tactics. This book will help you do all of that and more.

Think of it as a bigger boat.

WINNING

THE PROFESSIONAL

SERVICES
SALE

PART 1

Connect

CHAPTER 1

Seven Realities of Selling Services

Filmmaker Woody Allen reportedly once said, "80 percent of success is just showing up."[1] If that aphorism were true about selling, there would be little need for the countless books, seminars, web sites, and software programs that claim to be vital to sellers' success. Especially when it comes to selling services, you're likely to *lose* 80 percent of the time if you just show up. Imagine the advantage you would gain if your competitors believed that's all they had to do.

If you ask 10 successful salespeople how they land profitable work, you will *not* hear, "Hey, I just go and see what happens." Their answers *will* reveal consistent patterns of behavior that contribute to their clients' success and, by extension, their own. It's not accurate to call their behaviors customer-centered or client-focused, because that would imply that these sellers were, at some point, not focused on the client, which isn't the case. Instead, these sellers embraced the transformation of the seller's role to business adviser long before most people knew a transformation of selling was under way.

They also refuse to accept conventional selling wisdom at face value. Maybe there are cases, for example, when a client relationship is *not* the most important factor in a services sale. How can there be a list of hard-and-fast rules for selling services when each sales situation presents a unique mix of challenges, issues, and people? After all, today's winning "rule" can readily become tomorrow's relic.

Top sellers do share this goal: to deliver extraordinary value to their clients before, during, and after the sale. To accomplish that, they uncover what each client really needs and then use flexible, pragmatic strategies to chalk up wins for all concerned. Most of all, they understand the realities of selling services, and they use that knowledge to help their clients and themselves.

Sales Reality #1: You Must Prove Your Answers to the Three Burning Questions

Not all that long ago, services sellers rarely had to do much more than proclaim the greatness of their experience and promise to deliver results to make a sale. Naturally, even then this wasn't always sufficient. But often enough, competitive situations became battles of seller promises. And whoever made the most confident claims won.

Sadly for some, those days are gone. The "Assert and Promise" routine always made for a good show. But those who cling to this antiquated approach will watch their profits slip away. Granted, you necessarily make assertions during the sales process. What's changed is that you have to *prove* every assertion and show how you'll fulfill each promise—in detail. It doesn't matter whether your company is Global Galactic LLC or Two Guys in a Garage, Inc. You *must* back up everything you say.

Specifically, be ready to prove your answers to the three burning questions every client will ask (or is wondering about):

1. *Do you really understand what we need?* You have to demonstrate that you understand why the issue must be resolved and the implications of any solution you propose. You need to address risk and how you manage it, complexity, and the realistic level of client effort to get the job done. Clients expect you to take their preliminary ideas about how to manage a challenge and take that thinking a step further. Otherwise, why would they need you? To do that, you must grasp the issue with a degree of depth that allows you to speak authoritatively about resolving it. You prove your competence by conducting substantive discussions on the details of the issue. A superficial understanding will only get you into trouble and will likely lead to a sales process that veers off course. Your efforts to comprehend your clients' situation send an important signal that you are thinking about their interests. That begins to build trust, which will serve you throughout the sales process and your client relationships.

2. *Can you do what you claim?* As you talk to clients about your capabilities, imagine them uttering silently to themselves that famous line from the movie, *Jerry Maguire*, "Show me the money!"[2] They're probably thinking about some version of that demand. Until

you prove what you claim, by whatever means your clients want, it's all puffery. Don't use an unproven claim anywhere in your proposals, presentations, or discussions with clients. Be ready with your evidence, even if you don't need all of it.

3. *Will you work well with us?* Expect clients to test whether you and your team fit with theirs. You don't have to be clones of your client's team, so ignore most advice about creating artificial rapport by pretending you're someone you're not. On the other hand, don't be tough to work with, either. Find the balance between being too aggressive and being a pushover, and check your ego at the door. Remember, you may answer the first two questions with flying colors, but fail this one and you're likely to lose the sale.

Besides seeking answers to these questions, clients will also try to gauge how much you care about what they're doing. Some clients will assume that your interests are self-serving, but people pick up on the true motives of others in time. Be patient. If you do really care, your clients will figure that out soon enough. If you don't, they'll know that, too.

How to Escape the Commodity Trap

Some sellers complain that clients view their services as a commodity, leading them to ask for lower and lower prices. If clients say or imply that they can't differentiate your services from those of others, what they're really saying is that they can't differentiate your ideas. And that shifts the competitive battle to something they *can* differentiate: price.

You can escape the commodity trap with the power of your ideas. That is, after all, what you are selling. Find the insights and innovative approach that set you apart from others. Clients want your ideas, especially ones they're not hearing from every other services seller. Communicate your best ideas to clients and avoid the commodity trap.

Sales Reality #2: Insights and Capabilities—Not Relationships—Close Sales

Suggesting that a strong client relationship is important to the services sale is like saying humans need oxygen to survive. Everyone knows that it's more comfortable, and often more beneficial, to buy from someone you know and trust. But it's easy to overestimate the power of those relationships, especially when it comes to selling services. The days of clients automatically handing work to their favorites went the way of the three-martini lunch. Even a multiyear client relationship doesn't earn you a free pass, and it shouldn't.

Overestimating the influence of a client relationship can lead to complacency and a lack of the pure hustle you used to start that relationship. Maybe the client returns your calls immediately and gives you an audience whenever you like. But that level of access should encourage you to work even harder to make an impact. Some service providers check in with their top clients and use the time for informal conversations about the client's issues. If you're not ready to give your client two or three items of value for everything they share with you, that relationship will eventually lose steam.

Think about the first three meetings you had with your best client. Chances are that you prepared with intensity and looked for ways to bring original ideas your client could use. That's the behavior that got your relationship moving, and that's what will nurture it. Remember, the value of the relationship to the client lies in your ability to integrate your past experiences and your creativity to generate insightful guidance. Assume that the client holds you to a higher standard of performance than a new competitor, and you'll keep the relationship vibrant. Building relationships of mutual respect with clients gives any service provider an edge—if you take care of the relationship. But relationships take you only so far. They may open doors for you, but don't assume that past client relationships will also close sales.

Sanity Check: Maybe the Client Doesn't Want a "Relationship"

The conventional wisdom is that you should pursue trust-based relationships with every client. While that's generally good advice, some clients don't want or need a relationship with you. They are perfectly happy with mutually productive transactions with you and have zero interest in taking it further. Don't be offended if a client doesn't want to pursue a long-term relationship, and don't assume that the client is not right for your business for that reason alone.

Sales Reality #3: The Client Buying Experience Trumps Sales Techniques

Think about the last time you bought a small electronic product like a calculator, watch, or a data storage device. Chances are the product was encased in thick, molded plastic packaging, with no visible way to free the product—except maybe a hacksaw. That packaging makes the seller's life easier, not the customer's. Such experiences influence buyers' opinions. Some people swear they'll never buy again from a company that makes it so difficult to use their products.

In that sense, the sale of a service is no different. Your client's experience in working with you has enormous impact on the buying decision. You want that experience to be the *opposite* of trying to pry open that hard plastic product casing. Your job is to create a buying process that works for your client, not just for you.

The concept isn't exactly radical: You and the client codesign a buying process together, which allows the client to learn, analyze, and decide how and when to buy. Instead of focusing on how to sell to the client, you work to identify and create the conditions under which the client is comfortable buying. How do you design a client buying experience? Ask questions.

For instance, don't assume that a client wants to see a presentation, call references, and then read a proposal. Offer alternatives for the client to learn about you. Maybe your client wants a series of small group briefings, an interview with the service delivery team, and a call of support from your boss. The possibilities are endless, but you won't know how clients want to buy unless you ask. And you'll get kudos for bringing up the subject.

Some sellers take this codesigned buying concept a step further by offering to help their clients solve some aspect of the current problem as part of the sales process. Maybe the client has questions about managing the prospective change or about how to decide which seller to choose. It's becoming more common for sellers to lend their expertise in these matters to make the client's life simpler and to create a positive buying experience.

No matter how your client wants to buy, you'll still undertake traditional sales activities such as identifying decision makers, positioning your services in a favorable way, and communicating why you are the best choice. You'll pursue the precise activities, though, in collaboration with the client, not according to some predefined sales process.

Sales Reality #4: Likability Is Overrated

Sales experts tell us that people buy from people they like, so we should get out there and get on the buyer's good side. Some claim that people *never* buy from someone they don't like. The unfortunate result of this perspective is that salespeople get caught up in trying to win a popularity contest. Naturally, you don't want clients to find you repulsive, and no one wants to hire a jerk. But trying to get a buyer to like you is the epitome of seller-centric behavior, and clients instinctively recognize it as such. When you try to steer attention your way, it diverts everyone's attention from the problem at hand, and that's not good for you, the client, or the sale. Robert Cialdini, author of the classic book, *Influence*, has this take on likability:

> In every sales training program, the first rule is that you have to get the buyer to like you. I think that's wrong. The first rule of sales is for you to come to like the buyer.
>
> When you feel sincere affinity and concern for someone, that person usually senses those feelings, and barriers go down. That's because you are much more likely to protect that person's interests, and so both sides win. Besides, you can't control what the person across the table feels about you, but you can control what you feel toward that person.[3]

If you are skeptical, ask any politician whether this works and you'll get eager nods. They know that they must convince voters that they are looking out for the voters' interests or they won't win the next election. The reality is that a client may like you, and may even enjoy having you over for dinner, but unless you like your client and behave in ways that demonstrate that, you may be unable to reach a level of trust that encourages that person to buy from you.

Sanity Check: Dump "Business Development" from Your Card

When you begin a sales meeting with the ritual business card swap, what message does the title on your business card send? Many sellers use the title, "Business Development Manager," "Account Representative," or something similar. Think about how clients view that seemingly innocuous title. It says that you are there to build *your* business. Look for a more client-focused title, or leave the title off your card entirely. Your client knows that you're there to sell. No need to make it any more explicit or create barriers before you even hear the client's first word.

Sales Reality #5: Your People Are Not Number One for the Buyer

Services sellers often claim that the key to winning is the people they propose to do the work. Some go so far as to say that their company's talented people are the ultimate differentiator. There's little doubt that individuals can sway a sale, but to suggest that it's the primary decision point ignores a simple reality of the sales process: Clients care first about the impact of your services on them; then they think about your people.

Your team does have to make a good impression, and perceived competence is central in selling services. But the people on your team are probably not your buyer's foremost concern. Consider, for example, the architect who blithely describes the process of demolition and reconstruction of a client's office space, or the lawyer who suggests that litigation is the best alternative to resolve a dispute. Reconstruction projects or protracted litigation may be just another day at the office for the architect or lawyer. But either can be a jarring prospect for clients, whose mental wheels are no doubt spinning about the impact of those activities on their businesses.

Your challenge is to view the problem as though it's the first time you have confronted it and the possible solutions. Then, discuss the problem from that perspective. Just because you know that a wall must come down, don't assume that anyone agrees with you. Take your client through the thought progression and reach the conclusion together. The conversation may take a little longer, but you will have differentiated your services and yourself. Once your client sees that, then the people you propose to deliver the service can make the difference between a win and a loss.

Sales Reality #6: Value Is in the Eye of the Beholder

No matter what you believe about the value of your services, it's the client who ultimately decides the sources of value. Some sellers are so sure of their own perceptions that they miss what's really important to the client.

That's what happened to Chris. His company helps clients tighten up security for their information systems. His message, that clients can achieve highly secured information systems at a reasonable cost, helped him generate enviable sales momentum. Chris was winning in the marketplace with his message. But when he proposed his services to a longtime client, he lost the sale to a lesser-known, higher-priced competitor.

The loss was perplexing. Chris's sales proposal was flawless, including his detailed assessment of the threat his client faced, a creative strategy for mitigating that threat, and the six-figure estimate of value the program would deliver. He reviewed his hand-delivered proposal with his client sponsor and it was well received. Chris thought everything was in place—a high-value proposal, a trusted client sponsor, and the track record to make it all happen.

Why did he lose this seemingly sure bet? Chris got beat on his analysis of value. He made a compelling case for the overall financial value, but he missed the importance of one deal-breaking detail. The client was intent on training his own staff in conducting information security reviews, but Chris's proposal made only a passing reference to that priority. His competitor made the client's view on that point the centerpiece of the proposal and walked away with the deal.

You may think that Chris didn't listen to his client and that's why he lost. But Chris demonstrated that he heard the client by making reference to enabling the client's team to become self-reliant. Unfortunately, he didn't emphasize that enough; he stressed what *he* thought was more valuable, not what really mattered to the client.

You may understand how vital a credible expression of value is to winning the services sale, but keep in mind that the client is the final arbiter of value. Don't be surprised if you see value in a completely different light than your client does. When you are trying to come up with an expression of value, rely on the facts you gather during your interviews, and don't let your preconceived notions cloud your judgment. As Chris's case demonstrates, a superior understanding and expression of value can edge out a formidable opponent with a long-standing client relationship.

Sales Reality #7: Not *All* Sales Techniques Are Bad

Experts are always hyping various sales techniques as the guaranteed way to win. They have urged us to use a sales script, build "instant" rapport with buyers, ask inane questions about their worst nightmares, find their "pain," perfect an elevator pitch, read body language, ask for the sale, and always be closing. The latest rage is to advise salespeople to abandon their sales techniques to close more sales. Supposedly, today's clients have seen all the sales techniques and are immune to them.

It's clear that some techniques, like the high-pressure close, have no place in the services sale. And it's true that clients are on guard against slimy tactics the moment any salesperson contacts them. So falling back on annoying techniques, though presumably designed to help, can be bad for your prospects of winning the services sale. But be selective about which techniques you keep and which you throw away. Dumping all your sales techniques is as counterproductive as trying to diet at an all-you-can-eat buffet.

No matter what client situations you face, you still need to know how to conduct a sales meeting. That means you have to be able to open a dialogue, guide a discussion of the issues, and end the meeting appropriately. And you still have to persuade people to do business with you, so be sure you know how to negotiate and close the deal. Instead of labeling all sales techniques as bad, rethink how you communicate with clients throughout the sales process

Don't waste your client's time on gratuitous compliments, but focus on the substance of the issues. Drop the presumptive closing techniques and concentrate on reaching a mutually agreeable solution. Forget about creating superficial rapport and instead build a relationship based on your competence to tackle the problem. Instead of relying on techniques to push to a close, use your insights and value—the ultimate selling techniques—to pull your clients to a solution they want to buy.

Reality-Based Selling

If the realities of selling services tell you anything, it's that buyers want more from services sellers. They demand insight, not sales technique, and problem solvers, not vendors. Some people may suggest that responding to these realities is a sales training issue. But it is more than that. This market shift means redefining and expanding the traditional role of the seller. And that calls for sellers to change their approach to sales, beginning with how they prepare for their first sales call or meeting with a client.

CHAPTER 2

Before You Call (or Meet) Any Client

Stan hardly fits the rainmaker mold. Often disheveled and not very smooth, he has just enough social skill to survive the office holiday party. You wouldn't think he could sell anything. Yet Stan accomplishes what most other sellers only hope for. He converts the most improbable sales opportunities into qualified leads and wins a high percentage of those sales. Even more impressive, Stan also has a knack for turning up new sales opportunities, which he manages and closes like clockwork.

Some people attribute Stan's stellar results to his ability to woo clients in sales meetings, but Stan's success is as much about what he does *before* meetings as anything else.

Think Second Impressions First

Conventional sales wisdom suggests that a buyer's initial impression about a seller's grooming, demeanor, and body language make an indelible impression that will make or break the sale. If that were the case, Stan would be pumping gas for a living, not selling professional services.

Initial impressions matter, but most buyers are discerning enough to look past a fashionable suit and polished shoes to find what they're really looking for: unquestioned expertise and competence. They may ogle your expensive pen and leather portfolio, but they care most about what you know and how that knowledge can help them. Many buyers will form an impression based on superficial observations, but most won't make up their minds until you open your mouth and show them what you can do.

That's when they form their second impression, which is based on their perceptions of your competence. And that impression can certainly decide the fate of the sale because, in most instances, a client's second impression trumps the first one.

So, establish that you really know your stuff, and do that as early as possible. Most clients in the market for a service provider want to see two capabilities immediately. First, that you have relevant subject-matter expertise, and then that you, or your company, have the ability to handle their problem. If buyers don't have complete confidence in your capabilities, they may still ask you to submit a sales proposal; but don't expect to win the work.

Stan's success proves the point: He knows everything there is to know about doing business in India. Between his meetings, he works hard to stay on top of that difficult subject so his clients don't have to. And clients have to spend only 10 minutes talking to him to recognize the depth of his expertise, both in theory and in practice. Any superficial considerations about Stan's looks fall by the wayside.

Not that you should ignore appearances when you go to any business meeting. But don't bank on good looks and fine accessories to take you very far in the services sale. If you're brushing up on anything before that next client meeting, make it your subject matter, your knowledge of the client, and the capability of your offering, not your wardrobe.

Dump the Elevator Speech

You've probably been in meetings where the moderator asks people to introduce themselves and tell the group what they do. If so, you've heard the dreaded elevator speech. At some point during those introductions, these speeches blur together and start to sound the same. It becomes virtually impossible to derive any meaning from the vapid descriptions of what each person does for a living. When you're attending a networking event or a conference, you have to arm yourself with a short narrative about your business; but that spiel will often work against you if you use it in a sales meeting.

Chances are good that if buyers hear that your company "Helps you do more with less!" or that you "Help managers become better leaders, one employee at a time," you can bet the question rolling around in their heads is, "What time is this meeting supposed to end?" Not only that, once you've hooked someone with your elevator speech (as experts advise you to do), continuing in that vein diverts attention away from where it should be—on the client's issue or problem.

Even though a short elevator speech may seem harmless, it often delays a client conversation from getting to the point. So, if you really do help organizations develop their leaders, be specific when buyers ask about that service. You could use the first 20 seconds of an introduction to communicate how you assist organizations grow their leadership capabilities with professional development programs, recruiting, and retention strategies, for example. Then immediately shift the conversation to the client by asking what you can do for the organization.

When introducing yourself to buyers, base what you say on what you know about their organization and their issues. If you are aware that a buyer has concerns about employee retention, you should emphasize that subject in your introduction instead of trying to dazzle with a witty elevator speech.

The snappy pitch may work well for some businesses—retailers, for instance. A florist who is "Making the world greener, one plant at a time," may draw customers with that line. But the canned elevator speech doesn't work as advertised with services buyers, so spend your time preparing a custom introduction for each meeting.

Explore the Client's Buying Options

Before any sales meeting, you may be tempted to plot your approach to selling yourself and your service. Before you do, you must first understand how the client wants to buy. A common misstep in the sales process is that sellers push the sale too early and face predictable resistance from the client, who isn't ready to buy.

To smooth the path for a productive sales process, learn as much as you can about how the client wants to buy *before* you begin to sell. That way, you can design, in collaboration with your client, a buying process that aligns with how the client decision makers prefer to learn about you and your offerings. Without this step, you're likely to find that a standard process for selling won't match the client's needs, and you'll end up making extra presentations, arranging unplanned reference checks, or rewriting proposals. Instead, work with buyers to design a sales and learning process that works best for them.

Some buyers encourage sellers to give formal presentations of qualifications; others want casual get-togethers to learn about what you can do.

After outlining their objectives for you, some client decision makers then turn over the sales process to procurement executives. In some cases, buyers may want to make site visits to your previous clients, while a reference phone call works fine for others.

You won't find hard-and-fast rules for how clients buy. You can be sure, though, that as the complexity, cost, and expected value of the potential sale grow, so, too, do the length of the sales cycle and buyers' requirements for information.

As you prepare for initial meetings with buyers, brainstorm about alternatives for how the client might prefer to proceed. If you believe the client will view your eventual offer as complex and far-reaching, generate ideas to include as many decision makers and influencers as possible in your sales process. Perhaps you offer a webcast for selected groups of clients on how you'd manage a complex initiative for them. Or suggest a session on how decision makers can influence change in a project environment. If buyers are more likely to think of your solution as modest in scope but essential to the organization, you might be better off with small, in-person meetings.

You can't be certain what you'll learn once you meet with clients, but think through the possible options on how they might want to learn about your offerings. With those ideas, you can work with the client to devise a customized buying process to fit the situation. How clients want to buy should be the foundation of your eventual sales strategy, so make this subject a priority for your early meetings.

Prepare Thoroughly but Quickly

The French chemist, Louis Pasteur, said, "Fortune favors the prepared mind." He could have been talking about service sellers. Astute preparation is a must for every sales meeting. Clients expect you to make that effort, and it's a good way to show your respect for the time they agree to give you. If you show up for a sales meeting without adequate preparation, which some sellers do, you telegraph this message: "I don't care enough about you to spend my time understanding anything about your organization or issues."

Remember, buyers want efficient, fast-paced discussions of the relevant background information, so everyone can move on to the reasons for the meeting. The more time clients have to waste explaining the basics, the less chance you have to get to their pressing issues. Plus, if you don't study the basics before the meeting, expect your client to be justifiably annoyed. It doesn't matter how busy you are. Preparing well for every client meeting must rise to the top of your list—even if that means you have to drop something else. Keep in mind that the quality of your premeeting preparation will influence the quality of all your subsequent client interactions.

On the other hand, essential though it may be, meeting preparation can also reach the point of diminishing returns. Some sales training programs stress that premeeting preparation must be exhaustive. You're directed to spend hours scouring the Internet and other sources to find every scrap about the client's strategic plans. Of course you want to be thorough, but don't go overboard. Your goal isn't to become an expert on the organization; besides, you can't accomplish that using only secondary research, anyway. What you should aim for is a solid core of information about the organization so you can more easily absorb and react to what buyers add to the mix.

Facts Can Be Slippery

After the sales meeting had been under way for a few minutes, the seller slid a report across the conference table, saying, "Our analysis shows that your revenue per employee is falling, while it is growing for your primary competitors. We have recommendations to solve this problem." The client, recognizing the source of the data, pointed out that errors in the reported number of employees and revenue invalidated the basis of the seller's planned recommendation. The seller shrank back into his chair, and the conversation ended shortly after that. You'll never become an expert on the client's business by relying solely on secondary data sources. Look for the facts, but don't bet your sales effort on such data.

For an initial sales call or meeting, aim to complete your research in an hour or two. For complex initiatives, you may spend more time than that, but strive to assemble your base of knowledge quickly. The information you gather now about your buyer supports your initial meetings, and it will also be important to your ongoing sales effort. This background will guide subsequent client interviews and the design of your overall sales strategy.

You can start your preparation by creating six anchors, or a set of essential facts, about the buyer's organization: basic organizational structure, products and services, financial performance, primary customers, key competitors, and industry challenges. Most of this information is readily available on your client's web site or through search engines, especially if it's a publicly traded company.

TAKE A CLIENT SNAPSHOT

To build your background knowledge of a client's organization, organize essential information into six categories, or anchors:

1. *Organization profile.* What are the company's mission, size, number of employees, locations, corporate organization, years in the business, lines of business, and recent headlines?

2. *Major product/service offerings.* What are the primary product or service offerings? What offerings are contributing most and least to profitability?

3. *Financial performance.* Is the company growing? What are the dominant sources of revenue and profit? What is the financial forecast for the company over the next three years?

4. *Primary customers.* Who does the organization serve? Consumers? Businesses? Which customer segments are the strongest contributors to growth, and which are weakest or emerging?

5. *Key competitors.* Who are the company's chief competitors? Where are the competitive threats to the organization? Which companies are the toughest competitors, and are new competitors emerging?

6. *Industry challenges.* What are the key challenges the company and industry face? Has there been consolidation in the industry? Are there new market entrants?

Once you have the fundamentals, focus your attention on that part of the business you're hoping to work with. Do you have relationships with any executives in the organization? Do you know any of the board members? Have you worked for any of the board members' companies? Also, check for common customers, suppliers, or other services providers. You're gathering this information as a way to understand your potential position in the organization. During a sales meeting, you may have cause to mention a common acquaintance, so be sure you know where your relationships are.

Next, go through what you've learned to generate as many possible interview questions as you can. Your purpose is to develop potential lines of inquiry for the discussion. Look for trends in the information you've gathered and the impetus behind them. If the organization is growing, why is that happening? How has the company's competitive situation evolved? Are new company offerings in the works? Are the company's customers changing?

Once you have those lines of inquiry, turn your attention to the reason for the meeting. Generate potential questions about the buyer's issue, as you understand it. Use a simple framework, like the journalistic approach to creating a story: Ask yourself the six questions—who, what, why, when, where, and how—about the issue. For example, if a client calls to ask about assistance with improving the company's credit approval process, you might develop questions like these:

- What is the nature of the problem? What has been the impact of the existing credit approval process on customer ordering and cash collections?
- Who does the existing process impact the most? Customers? Accounting staff? Others?
- Why do you need to improve this process now?
- When did you first realize the need to change the process? How urgent is its resolution?
- How are you handling this problem now? Is there a workaround, or are you living with the situation as is?

Questions like these are diagnostic; they clarify what the client needs and highlight factors you must consider as you uncover the problem—and later for your sales proposal. The client's answers provide an initial look at the scope of the problem, its impact on the organization, and the need for resolving it.

The quality of your questions is one way you demonstrate your competence. In your meetings, be curious about the details, explore the implications of the matter at hand, and use your insights to frame your questions.

Don't fall back on trite sales throwaways like, "If you had a magic wand and could make everything right, what would you do?" Prepare questions that demonstrate your ability to hold your own in a high-value discussion of the buyer's problem.

Well-formulated questions almost always shake loose something interesting. You delve into areas that the client may not have considered, and that's when you uncover new opportunities. Jeffrey Fox, best-selling author and sales consultant, said of sales questions, ". . . being an expert is good, and you render that expertise with your questions. You ask questions that demonstrate to the client that you know what you are asking about. The Rainmaker always asks questions from which both people learn—the client learns from articulating the answer, and the seller learns by listening and taking notes."[1]

By asking the right questions, you find new ways to offer value to clients. Of course, as you pose questions, you should interject the relevant aspects of your experience. You may know, for example, how others handled the same issue or why the problem has emerged in other situations. But keep the focus on the client, not you. If you ever find yourself talking more than about 30 percent of the time, stop and listen for a while.

Finally, before you head into a meeting, always make sure you catch up on any new developments in your area of expertise. Scanning the recent literature before you meet a client is the least you should do. And if your company has new clients in areas relevant to the meeting ahead, be sure you are prepared to speak intelligently about them. Most buyers have lots of questions about their issues when they first meet you. Expect them to ask about the latest ways that others are addressing the matter, recent research on the topic, and creative ways to tackle the problem.

What Stan Knows

Some of Stan's colleagues marvel at his ability to capture buyers' attention and create value that often translates into a sale. But people who have spent time with him get it. Even if you don't aspire to greatness, you can learn a lot from Stan. For instance, he knows that his ideas are the basis of everything he sells. Bring the right ideas to buyers at the right time, and they will listen.

Work tirelessly to build your knowledge base. Most clients are too busy running their businesses to comb through the mountains of information out there, so do it for them. But never assume you can dazzle a client with knowledge alone. Before you set foot in a client's office, be ready with facts, questions, and options. Once a meeting starts, learn everything you can about the source of clients' problems and how they have considered addressing them. Clients should never think you are pushing a predetermined solution at them. And don't forget to find out how they want to buy.

Make a Connection

The secret to consistently generating new work is the buyer's belief in your competence and your ability to deliver value. You must also know how to manage a sales process, but you'll never get the chance if you can't connect with clients on the value of what you know and can do for them. In early interactions with a buyer, your ideas and the way you present them will sell for you. But if you press the sale before you've demonstrated your competence, expect resistance. Buyers will let you know when you've passed the competence test.

It doesn't hurt to make a positive first impression on your client, so dress well, carry a nice case, and take some time to break the ice. Just remember that appearance will take you only so far. At some point, early in your meeting, your client is going to form the all-important second impression about whether you know anything useful. And that second impression will determine whether you continue on with the sale.

CHAPTER 3

Master the Client Interview

I know nothing but the certainty of my own ignorance.

—Socrates[1]

Top professionals have this in common: They are very good at many things, but they *master* a handful of vital skills. Fashion designers must choose exactly the right fabric to fit a design; leading chefs worry about finding the perfect ingredients for every dish; and trial lawyers have to be persuasive orators.

Service sellers, too, must master a small number of high-impact skills to excel. Some experts argue that the top skill is closing the sale. Others believe it is the ability to deliver a knockout sales presentation or to write the killer proposal. No doubt, those are essential skills. But your ability to deliver that presentation or wining proposal or close the sale depends on the quality of the information you have to work with. And to get that information, you must be an expert interviewer.

Maybe you refer to interviews as *client meetings* or *sales calls*, but whatever you call them, it is during these interactions that you learn most of what you need to know to put together a winning service offer. Plus, from the way you conduct interviews and the questions you ask, buyers learn a great deal about your expertise and whether you and your company are equal to the task.

One of the chief reasons that some sales drag on and on is the poor quality, depth, and accuracy of the information a sales team gathers during interviews. If what you learn is incomplete, the rest of the sales process turns into an endless game of catch-up. As you try to work toward a solution, you'll find yourself pestering your clients with follow-up questions that you should have asked earlier. Some sellers forget the follow-ups and make assumptions about what they believe is true, hoping the client agrees to sort out the details later.

If, for example, you are proposing a training program for one division in a company, it would be foolish to make time and cost projections if you are unsure of the exact number of people who would participate in the training. By making assumptions about even the most basic facts, your eventual proposal loses clarity (and accuracy) and causes the client to wonder whether you really understand what you are proposing to undertake.

If you collect the wrong or incomplete information during interviews, flaws will eventually show up in your sales strategy, the proposed solution, your proposal, and sales presentations. Start with a wobbly foundation and everything you pile on top will topple.

You need to master many skills to become a great seller, but everything you do during the sales process will be more valuable to buyers, and will lead to better results for you, if you master the client interview. Become a great interviewer and you can become a great seller.

Six Steps to a Masterful Client Interview

Think of a time when a professional, say a doctor, a consultant, or an accountant, impressed you. What did that person do to create a positive connection? Probably, you sensed a high degree of professional competence, sincere concern for your circumstances, and an easy rapport. As time passed, you came to trust the person and felt comfortable sharing information. To achieve that level of trust, that professional had to know how to conduct a client interview.

Some people seem to have a knack for getting people to open up. But the reality is that it takes skill and a lot of practice to make interviewing look like second nature. To find your own interviewing style and to master this essential skill, follow these six steps.

Tune in to the Pros

The best interviewers hone their skills by watching experts in action. You can pick up more from a few hours of careful observation than you can from days of doing interviews by yourself. One place to start is to watch how people in the media conduct interviews. You can observe the best and the worst interviewers without ever leaving the comfort of your couch.

In 1977, British journalist David Frost used his considerable interviewing skill to entice Richard Nixon to reveal facts about his shattered career that no one thought possible. Talk-show host and journalist Barbara Walters regularly wrings tears from her interviewees on national television. But she does it in a way that makes guests line up to talk to her.

You don't need (or want) your interviewees to reveal their darkest secrets or break down, but you can learn what works and what doesn't by watching the pros. Notice how they probe from multiple angles to draw out the salient issues. Often, they'll ask essentially the same question with different phrasing to pin down a point.

Also, watch how they handle reluctant interviewees. Politicians and their spokespeople, for example, are famous for saying whatever they like, no matter the question. Notice the different methods interviewers use to elicit the responses they want. Sometimes they ask direct questions. Other times, they may read a quote from another expert or a passage from a report to get an unscripted and revealing answer.

Watch others for clues about what would work—or not—for you. Be careful whom you emulate, though. The media is full of softball interviewers who immediately move on if they sense the slightest hesitation about their line of questioning from their guests.

As you evolve your own style, keep three things in mind. First, a single interview style won't work all the time. You need to size up each situation and individual before you launch into your questions. So it makes sense to learn as much as possible about your interviewee before your meeting. At a minimum, you should figure out whether the person will be friendly or uncooperative. If you don't, you might get blindsided and walk away without the information you need.

Second, be amiable without fawning over the person. That doesn't mean being disingenuous or looking the other way when you don't get an answer. And it does mean not being arrogant. Obviously, you need responsive answers, and sooner rather than later. But that doesn't mean you push the person to drop everything to see you right away. Keep in mind that clients' need to do their jobs outstrips your need for information to support a sale.

Most important, don't just mimic others. Look for techniques that you can use, but integrate them into your own style. A strong sense of self is the reason many of the great interviewers succeed. Rely on what fits your personality and approach. When it's clear that you're comfortable with your interview style, clients are, too.

Break the Ice Quickly

Anytime you meet a buyer for the first time, some uneasiness exists for both parties. After you've exchanged pleasantries, make your purpose known quickly. Spell out any ground rules that you want to adhere to, especially how you'll attribute the information you're gathering and whether the interviewee will get a chance to see your findings before others do. Be sure to give the other person an opportunity to change the rules. By taking this small step early in the interview, you set the tone for a forthright discussion.

Know What You Don't Know

Before heading into any interview, you need a foolproof method to sort through what a buyer will lob at you to make sure you get what you need. Being a good note taker helps, but it's not enough to make the best use of the person's time. One simple technique is to think through, in advance, some hypotheses that might explain the client's problem. From those preliminary judgments, assemble questions to guide your interview. You're not solving the problem—just getting organized to make the most of your opportunity to learn what's happening.

For example, assume you are gathering information to assist a client in reducing customer order delays. Based on what you know, come up with a list of 10 possible reasons for the delays in customer orders. Your list might look like this:

- Staff absenteeism is creating work backlogs.
- Information systems reports are late or inaccurate.
- There's not enough order processing staff.
- There is high staff turnover in key positions.
- Order processors lack sufficient knowledge.
- Warehouse productivity is poor.

- There are too many customer communication snafus.
- Inventory shortages are a problem.
- Transportation and shipping problems abound.
- There are customer inventory management issues.

Your list may not be complete, or even right, but it's a start. Now compile questions for each area on your list to evaluate your preliminary assessment. You might ask questions like these:

- What is the current level of staff turnover in the order processing department, and has it changed recently?
- How does the current staff level compare to the past? Is the number of people working there higher, lower, or about the same as six months ago?
- Has staff absenteeism been higher, lower, or about the same as in the recent past?

Creating questions with hypotheses in mind gives you a systematic way to develop your thoughts about the range of possible causes for the order delays. During your interviews, test your hypotheses, get the facts, and begin to narrow down the reason for the trouble.

Don't expect to test every hypothesis, and don't worry if you have more questions than you can ask in the allotted time. You're likely to find the root of the problem long before you get to the end of either list. Your goal should be to open your mind to all of the possibilities before you start asking questions.

Even if you walk into an interview with pages of questions, you will have a few must-ask ones in your stack. Maybe you need to understand how an upcoming reorganization will affect the company, or what plans the company has for growing a product line. Separate those questions from the others, and don't become sidetracked by the discussion and forget to ask them.

Get Close to the Problem

As you plan for interviews, remember that those who are closest to a problem usually have the best view of it, and they may not be the same people who are hiring you. Broaden your view by getting as close to the problem as you can. The executives on the thirty-eighth floor know there's a problem. It shows up regularly on their reports. But they have only a bird's-eye view. Talk to the people who work in the storeroom, on the loading dock, or on the plant floor to find out what's really happening. Ask for advice, opinions, and facts. You want a mix of opinions, from across the organization, before you settle on an answer. Don't skip anyone who can help you.

When you're deciding whom to talk to, try a bottom-up approach. Begin with people on the shop floor, for example, and work your way up. You'll round up a lot of details this way, so when you meet with executives, you'll be ready with insightful questions. Don't try to rush the process, either. Some sellers want to blitz through interviews as fast as humanly possible. Speed matters, but comprehension comes first. If you find yourself doing more than four one-hour interviews a day, it's too much.

Where Shall We Meet?

You may not always have a choice, but if you do, try to find a location to meet other than the interviewee's office or work space. It's important to see where the person works, but getting the person's full attention may be impossible in the office. Suggest a conference room, coffee shop, or some other location where you can both relax and focus on the meeting, without interruptions.

Avoid This One Mistake

Leafing through his interview notes, Eric stared at the lines, arrows, and keywords that filled the pages. But he sensed that he was missing something important. During the interview, he certainly learned a lot, but he didn't have enough detail. From the information he had, he could not construct a complete picture of his interviewee's area of responsibilities, which he knew he had to have.

Eric's predicament is a common occurrence. You feel good when you wrap up an interview, but later find holes in the information you need. Many interviewees keep the conversation at a high level for fear of swamping you with detail or having to spend the afternoon explaining every last nuance to you. It's your responsibility to find the middle ground between generalities and minutiae. Sometimes you need the smallest details to understand the biggest issues or you'll be back asking obvious follow-up questions.

Be an engaged listener throughout your interviews. Ask your questions, listen to the answers, and then follow up. When you pose a question, wait quietly for the answer; don't feel you have to jump in to fill the silence. Ask for data, stories, and examples to support the points your interviewee is making. When you have doubts about facts or assertions, seek clarification. Check whether there are others you can talk to who can make sense of what you're hearing.

Unverified facts can turn a promising sales proposal into a nightmare, especially if the facts turn out to be wrong. Remember the old saying, "When in doubt, leave it out." More than one sales team has learned this lesson the hard way. The last thing you want is for buyers to ignore your proposal and take you to task over disputed facts. If a buyer challenges and disproves even one fact, all of your hard work can unravel in an instant. The solution: Verify everything with two sources. You should welcome spirited discussions with clients about solutions, but arguments over facts take everyone's eye off the ball. Make sure every claim can stand the buyer's scrutiny, or leave it out of your offer.

Before you consider any interview complete, check your notes and make sure you have those must-have answers. And, even if you have no doubt about that, ask for permission to call with follow-up questions. Most people will agree, so if you need to call it won't be a surprise.

Lost in Translation

When you enter your client's world, expect the jargon to fly. Every organization uses its own shorthand, and most people are not totally conscious of it. Don't take anything for granted. If a term or acronym is unfamiliar, ask for a translation. And be careful with your own use of jargon. When both the buyer and the seller are using their own jargon, misunderstandings are sure to result.

Resist Pitching

When you're sitting across the table from a prospective buyer, the subject of you and your services is going to come up. Most times, the buyer asks about what you can do before you kick off an interview. You have to answer, of course, but keep your "commercial" brief; what you say and how you say it can make or break the success of the interview.

A sales trainer may tell you that clients' questions and objections are buying signals, which you should jump on immediately. But sometimes, questions and concerns are just that, not a green light to put on the full-court press. Objections show what the client is worried about; they may be the opposite of buying signals and point to serious obstacles to the sale.

The best interviewers stay attuned to the task and resist the urge to sell. Instead, start collaborating with clients from the outset of every interview. Steer the conversation away from yourself, your services, and your company to address the details of the client's issue. You might think of client interviews as selling's equivalent of a demilitarized zone—no direct sales pitching allowed. That way, the buyer will be able to evaluate how you work. The quality of your questions and insights will add to the client's perception of your capabilities and to the relationship.

Although your aim is a peer-level give-and-take, let the client do most of the talking. What should you be doing? Plan to prove yourself with the relevance of your comments, not by taking the floor. And listen actively so you *hear* what the client is saying. According to the recent RainToday.com report, *How Clients Buy*, buyers think services sellers are not very good listeners: Of survey respondents, 38 percent cited "Service provider did not listen to me" as a major problem with sellers. And 55 percent of buyers said they would be "much more likely" to consider hiring the provider if the person listened better.[2]

You don't have to rely just on nodding and making appropriate noises to let buyers know you are listening. Clarify and summarize what you hear. Take notes on significant points. Make sure you have a reliable way to capture details that may be important later. Ask questions that make the other person think about the problem in new ways. Stick with the issues, resist pitching your solution, and listen. Those actions will help build a bridge of trust between you and the buyer that will move the sale ahead.

Start with Your 10 Best Questions

When you are facing a client interview about a complex business problem, what is the best way to draw out the information you need to make sense of the challenge? If you've done your homework, you probably have a long list of possible questions. But go in with 10 (or fewer) predesigned questions that you believe will elicit the information you need and suggest additional questions.

Ten questions isn't a strict limit, but rather a guideline to narrow down your thinking as an interview gets under way. After a few minutes with someone, you can usually sense which questions the individual can and can't answer. So selecting the right 10 questions means targeting your inquiries to areas you believe the person knows the most about. And then, don't make your questions so complicated that your interview turns into a walkabout.

Instead, begin with the facts. For the most part, fact-based questions (e.g., "How many people work for you?" "How many products are available in the European division?") get an interview rolling in a non-threatening way. You start to establish rapport and set the pace for the interview by leading off with factual, easy-to-answer questions. Think of this background as the foundation for the story you're building for later.

Sanity Check: There *Is* Such a Thing as a Dumb Question

Conventional wisdom tells us that there is no such thing as a dumb question. Supposedly, the only dumb question is the one you have but don't ask. In client interviews, you can get away with asking dumb questions—up to a point. But you better be a quick study or you'll be out of the running. Clients expect you to learn fast, and they will evaluate you on that basis. If the depth of your questions doesn't increase with each one, don't expect to have the client hand you the sale. Learn how to ask elementary questions in a smart way, and limit them to as few as possible.

Of course, you need far more than background to design a solution and prepare a compelling sales proposal. Once you grasp the basics, switch to explanatory mode to clarify the challenge the client faces. Assume, for example, your client wants to reverse a slide in high-talent employee retention. Your initial questions might be similar to these: "What is the current retention rate for high-talent people?" "How has that trend changed over time?" "What is your strategy for keeping your best employees?"

From there, explore why employee retention problems exist. How do salaries for top performers compare to others in the industry? Have employee satisfaction scores dropped? What is the trend in bonus allocations? Are there any new employee career path options? The hypotheses you generated before the meeting should guide your explanatory questions. The answers you get may eliminate or confirm your hypotheses or may add new ones.

In addition to eliciting factual answers, you should also tap into your interviewee's experience to build a better story and to take full advantage of all the knowledge that person has. Once you've gone through the person's perceptions of the facts, move on to appraisal and envisioning questions.

Appraisal questions allow you to find out people's opinions and assessments of the facts. You can get at these opinions in two main ways: directly or with a third-person premise. Direct appraisal questions ask for the client's personal point of view. You might ask, "Why do you believe certain high-talent people left the company? Or, "Why do you think the people you know choose to stay?" Keep your direct appraisal questions open-ended, but specific. Avoid asking for too much at one time (e.g., "Can you name seven reasons why the best people leave?"). Many interviewees will lose track of their own thoughts trying to answer questions that are too broad in scope.

Often, you glean even more by posing appraisal questions that ask people to step out of their roles and see the problem from someone else's perspective. You could ask, "If you were one of those high-talent individuals thinking about leaving the company, why would you choose to stay or go?" Sometimes, people are more candid when discussing the problem from the third-person point of view, so be ready with a few of those questions. Before using them, though, assess your interviewee for receptivity to this line of inquiry. More than one seller has asked such a question and gotten the response, "How would I know? Go ask the person yourself."

Another choice for appraisal questions is the compare-and-contrast kind, which ask the person to assess some aspect of the problem by comparing the current state with performance in the past. Use this approach to get a sense of how urgent the buyer thinks the problem is. You might ask, "If you were to look at your company's performance in retaining top talent today, how would you compare and contrast that to your performance on this measure three years ago?"

Once you've gathered ideas about why the problem exists, take your questions to the next level—envisioning. Ask the interviewee to reflect on the problem, offer opinions on potential solutions, and speculate about future possibilities. Stimulate thinking about the future with questions like, "If we were sitting here two years from now discussing this initiative, what would we say was our best decision?

✓ Envisioning Questions	
Good envisioning questions ask your interviewee to imagine looking back on the project from the future. For example:	
If you were to look back after two years, what would you say . . .	
Perception	**Issue Addressed**
Was the highest barrier we scaled?	Organizational change
Was the most valuable part of the undertaking?	Expected value
We should have planned for more effectively?	Risk and complexity
Was the most important change in the way people work?	Organizational impact

Projecting into the future offers a glimpse into the buyer's expectations for value from the service you're discussing. For example, you might ask, "If we were discussing this project in two years, what would we say was the biggest benefit you gained as a result?" Use your imagination to come up with insightful, future-based questions that challenge your client to think about the problem and its solution. Don't confuse these with generic sales questions like, "What keeps you awake at night?" Instead, study your preliminary hypotheses about the client's problem to generate useful, future-based questions.

To wrap an interview, consider a final envisioning question to put the client's views into perspective and maybe trigger new insights. Ask a "what one thing" question, which you can pose any number of ways. If you were anticipating a difficult transition, for example, you might ask, "If you could give me one piece of advice about managing change in your organization, what would it be?" Or maybe your goal is to reduce costs while maintaining a sense of teamwork. In that case, you might ask, "If you had one piece of advice for balancing the need for cost reduction and the priority for keeping productivity high, what would it be?"

When you ask a "what one thing" question, you'll probably get more than one answer—at least from most people. But let the person talk. Closing an interview this way makes the person concentrate on the subject. Keep your pencil handy, because you'll get some revealing answers with these questions.

There are dozens of variations on client interview questions, so open the faucet of your creativity and let it run. Remember, if you uncover just one nuance about the proposed assignment, whether it's about the specific issue or potential barriers to completing the project, you have the basis for crafting a differentiated, winning proposal. And that makes the hard work of preparing for an interview worth all of your effort.

Perhaps the biggest challenge you face during your client interviews is being certain that you've actually found the cause of the problem and that you can take care of it or, more important, that the problem the buyer wants you to solve is, in fact, the real trouble.

CHAPTER 4

Uncover the *Real* Problem

The greatest challenge to any thinker is stating the problem in a way that will allow a solution.

—Bertrand Russell[1]

P rofessional services companies sell their ability to help grow clients' businesses, whether that means solving a problem or supporting an initiative to boost performance. But their own profitable growth depends on solving the real problems, not just the perceived ones. Many clients are good at diagnosing their own problems and do extensive analysis before seeking outside help. But often they are mistaken and inadvertently lead sellers, and themselves, into a cul-de-sac.

Take the example of the executives for a financial services company who blamed poor customer satisfaction ratings on the lack of accurate information about customers' accounts. After studying the issue, the executives concluded that an overhaul of their complex information systems would solve the problem and put the information they needed on their desktops. Plus, an investment in new technologies would allow the company to reduce spending on expensive staff that supported the older information systems.

The solution seemed so straightforward. And several service providers stepped up to offer their services to make the proposed solution a reality. One seller and her team, though, looked more objectively at the matter through a series of interviews with key client managers. They found plenty of evidence to support the executives' conclusion that a system modernization was the way to go. But they also heard from some internal experts with dissenting opinions, who are usually floating around in most organizations.

After weighing the validity of the divergent opinions and completing their own assessment, the sellers proposed a scaled-down solution. Their proposal defined the problem differently than their competitors had, and they showed how the clients could achieve their objectives faster, with less cost, and with a higher probability of success than the original system overhaul plan. The client accepted the logic of the sellers' scaled-down proposal and hired them to do the work. The winning team's effort to understand and verify the real problem led straight to a high-margin sale.

Whether a client wants a professional development program, needs to integrate the operation of a new merger partner, or seeks to enhance company security, the services sale is a response to some kind of challenge. Buyers routinely tell you what they want to do and then ask, "Can you help?" In response, many sellers listen patiently until they hear that question, then launch into a sales presentation.

The rush to talk about your services forces you to promote *how* you can help before you are clear on *why* the client needs that help. As soon as the conversation turns to "how," sellers fall right into their comfort zones—talking about their services. If you find yourself discussing how to solve a problem before you are certain of its cause, take a deep breath and start over.

Shifting into sales mode before you understand a problem's source will lead to trouble down the road. First, you may commit the unforgivable sin of the services sales: offering an incomplete solution or, worse, the wrong one. If a buyer says, "We need a series of training programs to boost plummeting customer satisfaction," for example, some sellers will obligingly head off and design the program. But what if the problem is due to internal mis-communication or poor information systems support, not lack of training? If the real culprit emerges after you suggest an unsuitable solution, you lose credibility and damage the client relationship. And it won't matter one bit if the client agreed with your initial, flawed assessment of the problem. You will still have a lot of explaining to do.

Sanity Check: Client Problems Are Rarely Simple

Whatever a buyer tells you, business problems are rarely as simple or innocuous as they seem. The notion of "low-hanging fruit" (i.e., problems that you can solve without breaking a sweat) is illusory. The client may tell you that resolution will be a snap, but the problem might still have the complexity of the Manhattan Project for those who are responsible for tackling it. File away what you hear about how easy any initiative is going to be. It's probably not accurate.

Not to beat a dead horse, but you will also struggle to put together a compelling sales proposal if you haven't nailed down the real problem. Your proposal will end up an uninspired rendering of your capabilities, and every part of it, from your description of value to the schedule, level of effort, and fees, will reflect only broad assumptions and the client's representation of the problem.

Finally, certainty about the problem allows you to (eventually) devise a workable solution and decide whether it makes sense for you to pursue the problem—and the sales opportunity.

Forget What You Know

Great services sellers are, by nature, problem solvers. But they also know from experience that first impressions can miss the mark. The instinct to hear about a problem and immediately envision a solution is part of how the brain works. Preconceived ideas are the inevitable outcome of experience, and we are all susceptible to them. For instance, your first instinct might be to douse a small fire with water. But depending on the cause of the fire, water could make it worse.

Maybe you think you have seen a problem a dozen times and know exactly how to solve it. Well, maybe you do. Clients admire those who can size up problems quickly, and that is a skill to cultivate. But if you can temporarily forget what you think you know and separate the problem from the solution, you have a much better shot at figuring out the best answer. Once you put aside your bias, don't be surprised if the source of the trouble turns out to be different than you first thought. You don't have to stifle the reflex to think about *possible* remedies; just hold those thoughts until you are sure.

Sellers are certainly not alone in rushing to judgment. Clients also have powerful motivations to get moving on a solution. Once a problem has risen to the level where clients seek outside assistance, they want action. And the seller, always under pressure to close the deal, readily agrees to kick into high gear. Everyone wants to get to the solution fast, even if some details remain sketchy. In the rush to an answer, though, are the seeds of failure. In the absence of objective analysis, you have only preconceived beliefs based on a potentially flawed representation of the problem. Once you start down that road, you are a prisoner of the same thinking that led people to believe that the Titanic couldn't sink.

The Extra Step

Time after time, sellers rely on the buyer's answers to just two questions: What is the problem? And what can or should we do to address it? That discussion results in a recommended approach to solving the issue, so the seller prepares a sales proposal and then pushes for its acceptance. You can differentiate yourself and your sales process by asking the most important question: What are the real *causes*, not just the symptoms, of the problem?

That question demonstrates your commitment to solving the problem, not just closing the sale. The client will probably welcome the question, take you up on getting to the answer, and eventually hand you the sale. For most services sellers, taking the extra step to get at the real cause is not a stretch. But using a systematic approach will save you a lot of time. To arrive at the factual basis for any problem, ask three questions:

1. What is the problem?
2. What is *really* causing it?
3. What can or should we do to solve it?

At the outset, you need to understand the clients' perception of the issue and what they want to see change. For example, assume your client, Acme Global Manufacturing, is experiencing a slowdown in cash collections, making it increasingly difficult to pay suppliers. The company's suppliers are threatening to cut off essential inventory shipments. These facts give you two significant story elements: the problem, which is sluggish cash collections, and the implications—potential supply disruptions.

To round out the plot, you would figure out what level of improvement the client needs for the cash collection process. Maybe you and the client determine that Acme's goal should be to achieve average cash collections of 45 days per customer. With that, you have an outline of the problem, including the challenge, the implications, and the goal. Now you can turn to the source of the problem.

Get to the Root

Finding the origin of a problem does not have to be complex or time-consuming. But the process is a critical step in your sales effort. The knowledge you gain supports every element of your sales process, including your assessment of the opportunity, the solutions you propose, and how you position your services in subsequent discussions with the buyer.

As you conduct your analysis, you are also building client relationships. Through fact-finding interviews and other meetings, you get a good glimpse of the organization, its people, and how they do their jobs. And they'll get to know you, too. That exposure is invaluable as you map out your eventual sales strategy.

Jumping into the fray of a buyer's organization to ferret out causes is hardly hazard free, and it often means poking into sensitive subjects, such as people's competence and job duties. If you move through this process tactfully and effectively, expect to advance your sale. Drop the ball here, and expect the buyer to send you packing. Remember, this is not the time to push for a specific solution, but to listen and observe.

Coming back to the Acme example, the way forward is to deconstruct the process that brought up the problem in the first place. That will give you ideas about what's really causing the problem. Assume that the client's collection process has three major components: reviewing accounts, contacting past-due customers, and collecting past-due balances. Scrutinize each step in the process, looking for potential points of weakness or failure. Perhaps the staff's daily reviews are inconsistent, or the customer contact script is ineffective, or the cash collection process is not keeping up. Once you narrow down the source, and the client agrees that you are on the right track, you can comfortably explore potential answers to the question, "What can or should we do to address the problem?"

Like the tale of the three blind men trying to identify an elephant by touch alone, you will get diverse opinions about why any problem is occurring. You need to hear those opinions and evaluate them, but eventually you need facts. Each time you hear a claim, ask for supporting data. If someone suggests that poor customer follow-up is causing the lags in cash collections, ask for the evidence. That proof could be in the form of a report, externally generated information, such as a research study, or by your own confirmation of what you learn. As mentioned in the previous chapter, be sure you don't base your diagnosis, or your proposed solution, on uncertain facts.

One effective way to probe causes is to follow the advice of Taiichi Ohno, the pioneer of the Toyota Production System. Ohno believed that every problem was an opportunity in disguise and that having no problems was the biggest problem of all. Whenever a problem emerged, he encouraged his engineers to ask "why" questions five times in succession. By persistently asking why, Ohno was confident that anyone could get to the root cause of a problem—and see the solution.

ASK "WHY" FIVE TIMES

Get to the root of a problem by asking five "why" questions, each building on the last. Here's a sample of how it might go:

CLIENT: We need to improve our warehouse staff productivity. Our customer service ratings have plummeted and customer complaints are mounting.

SELLER: Why are customers complaining?

CLIENT: Because our warehouse staff is unable to fill orders accurately.

SELLER: Why can't your warehouse people get the orders right?

WAREHOUSE FOREPERSON: Because the items we need are not always in the inventory.

SELLER: Why don't you have the right inventory?

WAREHOUSE FOREPERSON: Because the manufacturing plant doesn't send us the right assortment of products.

SELLER: Why doesn't the manufacturer send the right products to the warehouse?

OPERATIONS MANAGER: Because the sales forecasting system has never functioned properly. We have given up complaining about it.

SELLER: Why doesn't the sales forecasting system function properly?

SALES MANAGER: Because the sales forecasting team doesn't get forecast changes into the system fast enough to ensure the right production schedule.

SELLER: So, the problem isn't really with warehouse staff productivity?

Check Every Angle

As you dissect any process, be sure to cover all possible areas that could be causing the problem. You can learn about the nature of any process, system, or organizational issue by looking at the factors that allow people, processes, and systems to work well together. Evaluate strengths and weaknesses by taking a systematic look at each of the following:

- *Performance.* For most processes, clients have acceptable and un-acceptable levels of performance. In the cash collection example, that process was no longer performing up to the standard, and the client then sought outside help. Measure performance for each component of the process, such as the timeliness of contacting past-due customers or the response rate for calls inquiring about payment. Look for clues that add up to a pattern. Maybe you notice that cash collection performance declined as staff turnover increased, for example.

- *Integration.* Business processes rarely work in isolation. The cash collection staff must work with the credit and order management teams, for instance, to share information and complete their work. Breakdowns often occur in the communication between different, but related, parts of an organization. Maybe the collections people are getting inaccurate or late information. Or maybe they are not getting the information at all. Check out the behaviors and activities between groups in the organization for evidence of what is causing the problem. Many times, minor changes in how these processes integrate can lead to significant improvements.

- *Education.* Don't assume that people know the best way to do their daily work. With staff turnover and organizational or information systems changes, some people may not know about, or know how to use, all of the resources available to them. That can lead to gaps in their understanding of the process in question. People's lack of knowledge about a process often contributes to poor performance, but it is rarely the full explanation for the problem.

- *Suitability.* Sometimes a process is ill suited for its job, leading to delays or errors. One company outsourced routine inquiries from employees on internal human resource (HR) matters. The cost of the service to the company was low, but the quality, accuracy, and timeliness of the information was poor, causing people to make phone calls to HR with questions the outsourcer was supposed to handle. The net effect was to raise, not lower, the cost of providing HR information to the company's employees. The process looked good on paper, but it wasn't working for those who needed to use it. Common areas of investigation to assess suitability are the number of steps in the process, the time to complete tasks, and the quality of the resulting work.

- *Support.* Many process failures are due to unanticipated delays that stem from an individual's need for help with how to complete a task. If that support is unavailable or inadequate, problems are inevitable. Look closely at how the organization supports people in managing their work, including both the support for handling ordinary questions and exceptions. A process or system may break down simply because people are unable to get the answers they need when they need them.

- *Satisfaction.* A final area to examine is the level of satisfaction with a process. It's always instructive to ask those who work in the process, and those whose work it impacts, open-ended questions about the quality, timeliness, and accuracy of the process. The answers to questions about satisfaction may not tell you what the real problem is, but they can point your analysis in the right direction.

Understanding Problem Scope and Impact

To get at the scope and impact of any problem, ask the client questions such as:

- What are the three key impacts this problem has on business performance?
- Who else inside and outside the organization sees this as a problem?
- What would happen if the problem was left unresolved?

Finding a Solution

When you confront a problem, it may seem like knowing the source automatically leads you to the right solution. But the first or second solution you generate may not be quite right. Keep going, and find other answers, or variations of your original ideas. Some clients will resist additional brainstorming, but push back. Find the third and fourth answers, which are often the highest-impact ideas. Instead of relying solely on familiar patterns, use your experience as a guide to make yourself see what is *unique* about the current problem, and then apply your creativity.

As you work through the options, keep in mind that whatever solution you devise is likely to change before you finish delivering your services, maybe even before you close the sale. Just asking questions can alter the situation, so your solution may have to change in response. Maybe the client experiences staff turnover that alters the way work flows in the problem area. Or maybe the staff implements an interim solution before you complete your proposal. Expect changes in the client environment and in the nature of the issue you're tackling.

Whatever solution you end up advocating, it will likely create unanticipated issues that will also need your attention. When one service provider simplified work processes for a client, those revised work methods became subject to negotiation with the affected labor union when the labor contract came up for renewal. You won't foresee every snag that crops up when you change something in the client's organization, but you should work out what those potential problems could be.

Finally, organizational dynamics play a role in the design of solutions and the ultimate success of any program. If a client is asking you to challenge the status quo, you will likely also be challenging someone's previous action or agenda. It's never enough to know exactly how to solve problems. To deliver your service successfully, you also have to master internal political dynamics. Ignore them at your peril.

Oh, So *That's* It

Once you have nailed down the source of the problem, summarize your essential findings in a concise problem statement. This, by the way, is also the foundation for your sales proposal. Here's an example:

Acme Global Manufacturing faces the threat that three strategic suppliers will cut off shipments because of delayed payments for inventory. The company has concluded that improving cash collections will result in a stronger cash position and boost the company's ability to pay its suppliers as agreed.

To address this challenge, Acme must improve its cash collection rate by 35 percent to regain its level of past performance. Achieving that level of performance within six months will resolve the company's payment issues. To meet this goal, Acme executives will undertake a cash flow improvement project by revamping customer communication, streamlining customer account management, and providing more timely information support for customer credit decisions.

Obviously, this example is simplified, but you get the drift. Drafting a problem statement guides the thinking on what the client needs to do and forms the core of your sales proposal. The most effective problem statement is specific, measurable, action-oriented, and client-focused. It lays out the problem, its implication, and the solution.

To solve the real problem and devise the right solution, smart sellers see past what buyers *think* they need. When you attempt to address the wrong issue, everyone loses, with higher costs for you, lower value for the client, and strained relationships. Most clients welcome close questioning and gain confidence when you crystallize their thinking about an issue. Of course, you can't know everything about a problem until you try to resolve it. Your goal is to get as close to certainty as possible.

PART 2

Collaborate

CHAPTER 5

When It Pays to Walk Away

At 2:30 P.M. every day, the division general manager, Alan, would close his door. Everyone in his office knew the routine. Alan was going down for his power nap, and disturbing his rest could be a dangerous career move. Most days, Alan was up and around again in less than an hour. Other times, particularly when he had a long lunch, he would be indisposed for a good part of the afternoon.

On the verge of retirement, Alan's nap habit spoke volumes about how he ran the division. Besides demoralizing his staff, Alan's management style also wreaked havoc with the outside services providers he hired to help with company initiatives. Alan gave his internal managers responsibility for implementing those programs, but they had no vote in the decisions to hire outside help.

One team of providers showed up to start work without anyone on Alan's staff knowing when they were coming or exactly what they were there to do. The service providers had interviewed people in the division and conferred with them on the creation of a proposal. But Alan decided later to shift the project objective and neglected to tell his staff about the change in plans. It soon became obvious to the providers that this was not an isolated incident in Alan's fiefdom and that they had made a really bad sale. Even putting aside the time they wasted to get the program going, who would want to work in that environment? The client relationships were doomed from the start, and you couldn't count on Alan for support or guidance, because if he wasn't in a meeting he was literally asleep at the wheel.

A sale to an organization like Alan's may look promising, but it's just not worth the effort. Even the most diligent discovery process won't reveal all of an organization's secrets. The trick to avoiding a bad sale is to make a *conscious* and informed decision about whether to work with a client and to be ready, when warranted, to walk away with no regrets. Taking on lousy work adds stress to an already-stressful life; it endangers your health and that of your business. To stay sane and build a high-value services business, be as selective about the clients you work with as they are about choosing you.

Sanity Check: The Case against Bad Sales

The main drawback to a bad sale stems from your lost opportunity costs. As soon as you get sucked into a bad deal, invariably something far better comes along, leaving you to kick yourself for chasing such a loser.

Ill-advised sales have other common characteristics: Often, it takes longer than you expect to close the sale, and by then your profit margin is already slipping into oblivion. It also takes longer to complete the work than you'd planned. Bad sales eat up more of your resources than they should, and the client is rarely happy with the end result. You risk sapping the morale of the sales and delivery teams for little long-term benefit.

Choose the Right Clients

How do you decide which clients are right for you? For some, the very prospect of revenue provides enough incentive to take on almost any business. Given the pressure on sellers to make their numbers, a few stinkers will probably land on their books. And with some buyers, you won't know you made a bad sale until the work gets under way and the surprises start coming at you.

Still, taking pains to avoid the albatrosses and choose the best clients for your practice fuels your growth and defines your future. Your business is a reflection of your clients, and the perceived quality of your client list affects your ability to attract new business. Scroll through the client list of any services business and you'll know how successful that company has been and where it is headed.

Getting and keeping the best people and creating a culture of growth are all functions of the quality of the work you sell. Sometimes you have to walk away from promising opportunities in the short term to build your business for the long term. The best way to improve your sales closing rate in the future is to be especially picky about the sales you choose to pursue.

Before you agree to write a sales proposal or attend another sales meeting, take off your client-centric hat for a few minutes and think about your own business. Does the sale you are pursuing represent the best use of your time, and what are the potential sources of value for *you* from it?

Start with a hard look at your profit forecast. You will rarely find a high-quality services firm that is not also financially successful. Be sure you understand the profit impact of every opportunity before you commit resources beyond exploratory discussions.

Use a range of assumptions to evaluate your profit margin. At what point would the sale look like a bad deal? What must happen to reach that state? For example, if your profit margin fell by 20 or 30 percent, would you still want to win the work? Also, consider the likelihood for additional profitable business from the client. Will those future contracts offer reliable sources of profit? How certain are you that you can achieve your profit margins?

Although profit should not be your only motive, be sure to shy away from loss-leader assignments—low-priced or free introductory jobs that you hope will eventually lead the client to buy full-priced services from you. You have no guarantee that loss leaders will ever pan out; they are for losers. If buyers cannot see the value of your contribution except through free projects, they may never get it. Don't take the chance.

Find at least three reasons why you might choose to work with a client, and one of them cannot be, "I don't have anything else planned, so why not?" How might the opportunity change you or your business for the better? Consider the potential "Seller Sources of Value" to assess what matters most to you from the sale.

SELLER SOURCES OF VALUE

A specific sale might offer you the chance to . . .

- Achieve a desired level of profit
- Work with this client on other assignments that are in the works

(continued)

- Build a long-term relationship with a strategic client

- Obtain valuable referrals and references

- Improve your client base, enabling you to recruit and retain top talent

- Develop a new service for the market

- Increase industry visibility for your business

- Undertake challenging or leading-edge work that will aid in your professional development (or that of your team)

- Add to your store of intellectual capital for use in marketing or on other initiatives

- Gain valuable expertise for growing your business in new areas

Maybe the client is an industry leader that you have been itching to work with and you are exceptionally well qualified for the assignment. If you can make a high-value impact on the client's company or industry, that may be reason enough to pursue the sale. Maybe you can build a stronger network of contacts, or you can add to your qualifications in ways that will be indispensable for other pursuits. Whatever three reasons you identify, fix them in your mind and plan a way to accomplish each one if you win the work. If you cannot find three good reasons beyond immediate cash flow to pursue a sales opportunity, consider walking away.

Find Your Real Opportunities

Once you believe that the client is right for you and you know why, size up your chances to win the work. What are the odds that the client will actually hire a service provider? For any sale, you always face two tough, invisible competitors. The first is the client's own people, who may want to do the work themselves instead of hiring outsiders. The second is any unseen event, such as unplanned executive turnover or poor quarterly performance, that might cause the client to pull the plug and not do the work at all.

Donna, a strategy consultant, learned the lesson about invisible competitors the hard way. Donna and her small team arrived for the client meeting right on time, and a harried assistant whisked them into the conference room. The client executive was running late, they learned, but would be there soon. As Donna and her colleagues pulled chairs up to the conference table, one team member pointed to a pile of bound documents on the center of the table. Donna leaned across the table and saw at once that the top document was a competitor's proposal for the same work Donna's team was there to talk about. Curious, Donna shuffled through the rest of the documents, counting a total of four proposals. The client was talking to at least five service providers for this initiative.

The client and his team arrived for the meeting just as Donna finished straightening the pile of proposals. Then Donna and her people spent the afternoon hashing over every detail in their proposal with the clients, with special emphasis on the work plan. The clients were intently interested in exactly how Donna's team intended to do the work, particularly how to manage the effort across time zones, which Donna's team knew quite a bit about. The meeting wrapped up on a high note, but Donna knew the competition on this one was going to be fierce.

After a week passed without any word, Donna called the client to see if there was any news on the proposal. The client was unavailable. She tried again three days later with no luck. When the client finally called back, Donna knew the news wasn't going to be good. She braced herself, but was still blown away to learn that the client decided to undertake the work without any outside help. The winning competitor—the client's own team—had effectively outsourced the analytical and planning work to consultants, at no charge. Using the ideas and methods they gleaned from numerous meetings, the clients fashioned their own project approach and left the consultants holding the bag.

You can understand how frustrated the five teams were after they invested substantial time and energy to pull together thoughtful proposals, only to learn that the opportunity was not real. When clients don't play nice, anyone can fall into this trap.

The second invisible competitor can be as bad as the first. Sometimes, the client scraps plans in the midst of the sales process. Maybe a budget crunch hits, or a boss decides to rearrange company priorities. In such cases, you are competing against unseen forces. A client can, at any time, decide the whole idea just won't work and call a halt to the effort. Given the possibility that a sale may never materialize, keep your ears open for hints from the client. Assess the client's commitment to using an outside service provider at every step of the sales process. You make investment decisions each time you choose to pursue a sales opportunity, so use every available source of information to make sure you invest wisely.

Sanity Check: Seven Buyer Remarks You *Don't* Want to Hear

When you hear variations on any of these themes, you might want to leave the sale to someone else.

1. "We expect budget approval next month, but we want your proposal now."

2. "You will need to deliver your service a lot faster than that."

3. "We tried to do this once before, but the people we hired dropped the ball."

4. "We will name our manager as soon as we decide which provider gets the contact."

5. "Your competitor wrote the specifications for our request for proposals (RFP)."

6. "We have 12 proposals under review as of now."

7. "We are insisting on a fixed-fee, fixed-schedule proposal."

The four essential questions discussed next can guide your thinking about the viability of an opportunity.

Does the Project Have Funding?

In many companies, people other than your sponsor must authorize expenditures. If that's the situation, you want a green light from the holders of the purse strings to signal an intention to proceed. This has been a costly lesson for many sellers.

After a five-month ordeal, one sales team, for example, won a highly competitive sale against three strong competitors. The winning team members made numerous sales presentations in multiple cities; they dedicated a full-time proposal team to the effort; and they revised their proposal more times than they cared to remember. Fortunately, or so they thought at the time, they won the job. Later they learned that the initiative's sponsors had never secured funding. As the sponsors started the capital request process, the company's board made two announcements. First, the company's president was stepping down, and second, all capital expenditures would be on put on ice until the new executive team could make their own spending decisions. The "winning" sales team still awaits that decision.

Asking about funding can be delicate, but you need to know. Don't pop the question right after you sit down to talk, but don't leave the meeting without the answer, either. Use your good judgment to frame the question. You might ask about approval to proceed without explicitly asking whether the budget has the go-ahead. Or you can ask if there are reasons to expect a delay in the start date—assuming the client approves your proposal in the specified time frame. You may be convinced that the budget won't be an issue, but try to get some evidence. The funding status may not be a reason to walk away from a sale, but it offers essential insight into the client's priorities.

Are They Ready to Start?

Some buyers are fishing for information—like the ones who solicited five proposals with no intention of hiring anyone. You can assess commitment by getting specific about the start date. That conversation should arise naturally, as you clearly have a need to know that date to organize the sales effort. You are looking for an indication of the client's depth of thought on how the program will unfold.

Don't expect to get a definitive answer from one or two questions. You might ask questions such as: Do the client's people understand their upcoming roles? Have they released any communications about the effort? Have they given any thought to support staff or the other resources you will need? Have they thought about the schedule, the organizational impact, and the implications for their business functions? All of these topics offer an indication of readiness and whether the opportunity is a real one. If you get precise answers and a give-and-take discussion, you're probably in good shape. If the client responds in foggy generalities, you are likely still at the very early stages of the sales cycle.

Does the Client's Business Case Make Sense?

An anemic or nonexistent business case can derail an emerging program faster than you can say "When should we get started?" You don't need to see a 30-page cost-benefit analysis, but you do want to know two things: Why does the client want to pursue this, and why now?

For most services sales, the client sponsor must be an advocate for the value of the work. Even if there's broad agreement among client executives about the need for the program, the sponsor will usually need to reassure supporters and convince doubters. You can't know for certain if or how a business case will sway people in an organization, even if it convincingly outlines anticipated value. But you will know if *you* believe it, and that may be enough. Whether the client spells out the reasons behind a program in dollars and cents or in some other way, do you think those reasons are sufficient to compel action? If you find the business case to be weak or nonexistent, suggest ways to strengthen or create one that makes sense. Before you get too far into your sales cycle, be sure the client's business case supports the proposed action.

Nine Causes of a Bad Sale

If you have three or more of these issues with a sales opportunity, watch out.

1. Poor personal or team chemistry with the client

2. Fuzzy objectives or scope

3. Unrealistic client view of the schedule

4. Inadequate resources assigned to support the initiative

5. Poor definition of team roles and responsibilities

6. Lack of management support

7. Infrequent client communication

8. Shifting leadership roles among the client team

9. Unrealistic expectation of value

Does the Buyer Have a Rational Decision Process?

Often, the decision process to buy services is ad hoc. Because most services purchases are episodic, many organizations don't have a routine process for buying services. In some situations, a group of interested executives gets together to decide among themselves how they will buy. In other instances, executives decide on the fly who will win the work. Whatever the scenario, find out if a decision process exists and, if so, ask how it works. Don't be surprised if clients don't have a process, and don't give up if they can't explain it to you.

To judge the validity of an opportunity, you want some evidence that the buyer has thought about bringing the purchase decision to closure. The formality of that process doesn't matter. If a decision process doesn't exist, you should be able to offer a few alternatives for one based on your previous experience. Just remember that you can have broad consensus on the need for action, and a compelling sales proposal, yet still get bogged down for weeks or months due to the client's poor decision-making process.

Do the Right Thing

The decision to walk away from a sale is not just about you, of course. What's best for the client should be just as important. Craig faced a senior client team who wanted to hire his company, without competition, for a short but critical project. After studying the objective and scope of the proposed program, Craig let the client team know of his serious reservations about the advisability of the project. He was especially concerned that the project would address a substantial problem with only a temporary remedy—a Band-Aid in his view.

The clients were adamant about taking the approach they proposed, even if it turned out to be more costly in the long run. Craig stunned the clients by declining to take the work, because he believed it wouldn't be in their interests to proceed in the manner they intended.

Craig's decision to stand on his principles cost him a short-term sale, but it eventually landed him a long-term client relationship that resulted in a string of high-profit projects. The client executives knew they could trust Craig to watch out for their interests, and they hired his company repeatedly on the strength of his decision to do the right thing.

Go for the Work You *Know* You Can Ace

As part of your assessment of the opportunity, be sure in your own mind that you can *really* do the work as the client wants and needs. Pay particular attention to the client's expectations of value, objectives, timing, approach, and the team. You'll work with your client to finalize these details, of course, but expect the client's initial opinions to weigh heavily in the balance. Listen to what the client says about these important issues. Are there reasonable expectations about how long the project will take to complete and its expected value? Does the client have a realistic grasp on the level of effort required?

What you should learn from these discussions is whether you can work within the client's constraints. You'll also get a sense of how flexible your client will be about revising expectations should circumstances change during the effort. If it turns out that you and the client are not in agreement about how to complete the work, can you collaborate to arrive at an agreeable resolution?

What's the Level of Executive Support?

Without solid executive support across the organization, a sale and the eventual delivery of your services are not likely to turn out well. Change tends to cut across organizational boundaries, affecting the jobs of many. Even a new process and system for updating vacation schedules, for example, impacts nearly everyone in a company. Without commitment and cooperation at all levels of the organization, a seemingly simple project can fail miserably. For a big undertaking, the impact increases exponentially.

Accept that unanimous support will be elusive. No matter how innocuous the change, you can't please everyone. But key sponsors, plus those who can influence the outcome, must be with the program. You may have a perfect plan, the best team on the planet, and a business case to die for, but without the right support, you'll end up in the ditch. You can accomplish a lot even in the face of withering resistance. But it takes longer, becomes more difficult, and has a higher cost of delivery. Be sure you understand who is in your corner before you agree to proceed.

Can You Decipher Those Client Clues?

As the sales process moves along, watch for both verbal and nonverbal clues to the client's view of the proposed initiative. Try to identify any and all red flags. Your conversations should cover all the bases, including the client's opinions about the schedule, how you will deliver value, and what role the client's people will have in the work. Pay attention, and you can learn about the opportunity, your chances of winning it, and how the client sees the project unfolding.

What Don't You Know?

Once you have gathered this intelligence during the sales process, ask yourself, "What am I missing that might change my view of the sale? Consider all of the relevant factors. For example, can you implement the project as specified? Given the constraints on you and the client, is the schedule realistic? How will the client really benefit from the initiative? You may not fill in all your knowledge gaps, but you can decide which facts you must have and those you can live without. Use the list, "Ten Things You May Not Know . . . but Should," to jog your memory for additional data you may want to collect.

TEN THINGS YOU MAY NOT KNOW . . . BUT SHOULD

1. Does the client have any plans for reorganization? If so, how will those plans affect the proposed program?

2. Who are your competitors, and what's the nature of their client relationships?

3. Have the clients tried this project before? If so, how did that work out for them?

4. How would you characterize the caliber of the client's team? Do the team members have the skills to pull this off?

5. Once the initiative is under way, who will be your main point(s) of contact?

6. How does the sponsoring executive fit with the rest of the management team? Is the whole executive team supportive of the effort?

7. Do the clients work well with outsiders? How do you think they will respond to those who have responsibility but no ultimate authority?

8. Does the client have a good payment history?

9. Who negotiates contracts for the clients? Do they use procurement executives or other professional negotiators?

10. What policy does the client have on ownership of any intellectual property that might come out of this effort?

When to Walk Away

Aside from the obvious aversion to turning down a paying client, the hardest thing about walking away from a sale is that you will never be able to prove you were right. When you do walk away, you are making an educated guess. After sifting through all of the facts, listen to your instincts. If something keeps nagging you about the situation, go back through what you know one more time, or make some phone calls to your client contacts and colleagues and try to clear up your doubts. If that feeling of dread persists, walk away and don't look back.

CHAPTER 6

Five Elements of a Winning Sales Strategy

As Denny gathered up his presentation notes from the podium, he couldn't imagine how things could have gone any better. One by one, the members of the buyer's selection committee rose to their feet for a spontaneous ovation that would make any seller smile. Once safely out of the clients' earshot, the five people on the sales team didn't even try to conceal their exuberance. This sale was in the bag.

Everything went exactly as rehearsed. The two senior team members, Michele and Denny, did most of the talking. Michele led off with a summary of why her team was ideal for the assignment, moved on to a crisp recap of her company's deep expertise on the issue at hand, and closed by committing all their resources to a smooth delivery. Then she introduced Denny, her project manager, who hit every point with conviction and clarity. The facts and figures, illustrated with a series of charts, supported the team's assumptions, solution, approach, and schedule. Denny bolstered his argument with three case studies of previous assignments, glowing testimonials, and results from a survey showing that the clients' initiative would place them at the forefront of the industry. He finished with a confident reminder of why his team was the best choice the client could make. The team happily headed back to the office to await the decision.

When the client called, the news ruined the team's weekend. The sale went to a competitor with "slightly better" qualifications, or so the client said. In follow-up interviews, Denny learned more about the loss. In spite of the buyer's demonstrated admiration for their presentation, he and his team had missed one of the essential elements of a winning sales strategy: They failed to spark the clients' imagination about their future. The presentation was technically perfect, the sales proposal was error-free, and the client knew the team would do a decent job. But that wasn't good enough.

The winning sellers made an equally strong case for their qualifications, but they also created genuine excitement among the clients with their *story* about the client's future, which they emphasized during their presentation and throughout their sales process. The team also had a convincing expression of value for the project, including why it must be done now, not later. And they made explicit references to potential risks and how they planned to manage each one. Most of all, though, the client trusted the team, and that was the final deciding factor.

The winning team knew that a traditional sales strategy that mostly stresses qualifications can be impressive and yet still not compel buyers to take action. Instead of relying on that approach, the winners brought every part of their presentation, and their sales process, to life by incorporating into their strategy five distinct elements for all of their client communications.

FIVE ELEMENTS OF A WINNING SALES STRATEGY

1. *Compelling story*. Help clients see their destination, how they will get there, and your role in the story.

2. *Airtight case for change*. Convince clients why they need to make the change, and why now.

3. *Comprehensive view of value*. Along with the obvious sources of value, uncover unexpected ones.

4. *Mitigation of risk*. Take the reasons to say no out of the equation.

5. *Trustworthiness and trust*. Transform trustworthy into trusted.

Element 1: A Compelling Story

For as long as anyone can remember, people have told stories to teach, learn, keep history, and to entertain. Humans are storytelling creatures. A good tale disarms people and taps into their emotions. Natural defenses tend to melt away when you hear someone say, "Let me tell you a story."

The effectiveness of stories is not exactly a news flash. Yet, as soon as most people enter the conference room or the boardroom, say for a sales meeting, they leave their stories behind. Instead, they rely on fancy graphics, rows of numbers, and chart after chart to communicate. Data can be persuasive, but a compelling sales conversation must reach beyond the analytical and into the envisioning area in buyers' brains so they can "see" the future you're proposing. Stories are a much faster route to the imagination than data alone; together, they pack a real wallop.

Ed was one seller who knew how to tell a story. Several years ago, some U.S. states undertook large-scale projects to enhance their ability to serve the needs of children. To offer eligible children the right services at the appropriate time and to manage child welfare programs, government officials needed effective, up-to-date information systems. Service providers, especially technologists, bid on projects to help design and implement these complex tracking systems.

The competition for these projects was intense. Most teams took a typical approach: They framed the problem as a technology challenge and peppered their proposals and presentations with boasts of expertise in information system design, networking, database management, and a host of other technical skills. The competitors battled each other for position as the highest-quality, lowest-cost choice.

Ed and his team took a different tact. They started with their passion for helping children. Ed talked about how important the issue of child welfare was to him personally—that seeing the fate of neglected and abused children had compelled him to try to make the world a safer place for them, so much so that he decided to dedicate his professional life to this cause. He told clients how he had assembled a team of like-minded people and together they set out to make a difference. Ed was a man on a mission first, a seller second. And he got that point across with stories.

Of course, his team also got into the nitty-gritty details of systems, networks, and software. After all, that was what the clients needed. But Ed and his team never lost sight of the future they hoped to create. Keep in mind that these were highly competitive, public-sector projects, which entailed voluminous responses to RFPs, required strict adherence to rigid selling rules, and were biased toward the lowest-cost bidder. Over time, though, Ed and his team won a great many of these projects on the strength of their qualifications *and* their story.

If you want clients to hear your message, think about how you can use stories. Facts and figures are necessary, but inadequate. You don't have to be Mark Twain to weave the facts into an engaging anecdote. And your stories don't have to be long, grandiose, or heart-wrenching. For instance, don't just talk about how your proposed solution will allow a client to purchase raw materials more effectively. Describe how the life (and morale) of a warehouse worker improves when the number of complaints about lack of inventory is cut in half. Tell your client what the proposed change means for the people involved. How will their work lives be different or better? Sure, buyers want to hear about how your proposal will impact the facts and figures of the business. But there's more than one way to express that.

People perk up when they hear stories. It's a natural reaction. Don't be afraid to use them in your sales communications.

Element 2: An Airtight Case for Change

Change rarely comes easily to any organization, even with broad agreement that it's necessary. It takes more than desire to break through the resistance to change that exists in most companies. Take the iconic company, Kodak, for example, which dominated its markets for decades. When digital technology upended the world of film-based photography, Kodak faced the threat of massive market losses.

Kodak's brain trust hemmed and hawed about how to thrive in the new era until it was almost too late. Even after the market made the inevitable leap to digital, the company stood by, offering a digital camera that still used film. And it wasn't as though the digital revolution was a surprise. Kodak's employees developed the first working sensor for digital camera technology in 1986. Even with the advantage of knowledge, the company stumbled mightily.

Kodak's struggle proves that some people and organizations will routinely battle change, even from indefensible positions. As you work through your sales process, anticipate resistance to change from at least seven possible sources, as shown in the table, "Making the Case for Change."

A harsh reality of the services sales is that there are many more reasons for clients to say no to proposed changes than there are to say yes. The only way to break down the barriers to change—inertia, indifference, cynicism, and the like—is to overwhelm those tendencies with imperatives for making the change. Here's your chance to use the power of storytelling. Combining stories and data, paint a picture of the client's current state. Demonstrate why the client must change and must do it now.

Making the Case for Change		
A convincing case for change addresses seven organizational barriers:		
Barrier	**What You'll Hear**	**What to Do**
Inertia: Predictable resistance to any change.	"Why should we do this now?"	Contrast present to proposed future in terms of potential value.
Indifference: Failure to take ownership of the issue/problem.	"Not sure why I'm involved, but I'll go along if I'm told to."	Point out the impact on and ramifications for individual stakeholders.
Cynicism: Doubt that proposed change will do any good.	"We tried this before and the effort fell flat."	Illustrate the plan for achieving results.
Risk: Perception that proposed change has too much financial, operational, or personal risk.	"You want to do *what*?"	Acknowledge risks and describe your approach to mitigating them.
Cost: Concerns over known and unforeseen cost of the proposed service.	"There are just too many other budget priorities."	Create a compelling case for what the organization will gain.
Priorities: Belief that other projects, initiatives are threatened.	"So, we just pile this on everything else?"	Discuss strategies for managing disruption and managing the project.
Effort: Perception that the undertaking is too complex to complete.	"We'd have to hire an army to get this done."	Offer examples of how you have handled similar work in the past.

For example, some clients asked a service provider to help design operational improvements for their product distribution network. According to the clients' estimates, the costs for labor, transportation, and product returns were sky-high and getting worse. Just getting the right products to customers had become a challenge because of the growing number of new products the company was offering. Still, some of the client executives thought other issues were a higher priority. Most of them might listen to ideas for a better distribution system, but they would be a tough audience. After a contentious discussion, the client executives authorized a brief exploratory project to size up the problem.

A joint client and service provider team started collecting every available piece of performance data about the company's distribution network. The team members turned the company's information system inside out; they conducted interviews with the company's employees, customers, and suppliers. Within four weeks, they were ready to report their findings to the client executives.

The project team opened the meeting with a story about one of the client's biggest customers, which had recently shifted most purchases to a competitor. The team let the customer executive speak for himself by showing a video interview of him recounting his reasons for taking the company's business elsewhere. He talked about receiving the wrong orders almost 30 percent of the time, which in turn caused havoc with *his* customers.

The team then shared the findings of an employee group interview that explored how the poorly performing operation led to numerous snafus, disgruntled customers, and a backlog of product returns that were stacking up in the company's warehouses. Using the company's own financial reports, the team showed the squeeze on cash flow from all the product problems and that warehouse overtime charges were escalating.

Finally, the team turned its attention to the company's competitors. Using public records and other sources, they learned that the company's chief rival planned to lease substantial new railcar capacity over the next several months to transport products into the client's strongest region. Sensing weakness, the competitor was poised to grab market share. A substantial threat was looming—in the client's most important region. All of a sudden, the threat came alive for the client executives. Customer defections, soaring costs, and competitor intrusions brought the case for change into sharp focus. Collectively, they knew they had to act. And they did.

Sanity Check: Communicating the Need for Change

You'll usually find a disconnect in the way the people at the top and the bottom of an organization view the severity of any problem. What may be a clear imperative for change could ultimately be shrugged off as small potatoes by decision makers. Don't beat your head against the wall trying to be the primary advocate for change. Engage others in the organization. Let their voices and opinions be heard through video clips, quotes, and any other means that give strength to the arguments in favor of change.

The exploratory team knew from the outset that executive action wasn't a given in this situation. The company, like all others, faced numerous challenges, all of which were competing for attention and resources. The team's stories, which made every aspect of the problem real, spurred action. The facts were an important part of the case, but the team's presentation was anything but a dry recitation. Instead, it was a vivid recounting of the threat's seriousness.

When the team wrapped up, there was no doubt that the executives had to do *something*. And that point stirred a long debate, which was this client's first step toward change.

Element 3: A Comprehensive View of Value

Every services seller talks about value. In the world of sales jargon, client value has become the holy grail. And most sellers are quite capable of pointing out the obvious ways their services will produce value for buyers.

For example, if you are proposing to help a hospital reduce its inventory of medical supplies or to help a retailer implement a new financial reporting system, the primary sources of value are clear: Reducing the hospital's inventory investment should increase the cash available for other purposes; the retailer's new financial reporting system should, hopefully, lead to better funds management, which in turn could provide higher returns on idle company funds.

Impressive as these gains may be, clients usually hand these expectations of value to sellers on a silver platter. Competitors will take these known expectations of value, add data from the results of their past projects, and parrot back to buyers, in proposals and presentations, the value they will get. Where's the insight in that?

That's not to say you should ignore the obvious points of potential value. On the contrary, you must use all your analytical skill to quantify and qualify what buyers stand to gain. But push your assessment of client value beyond what everyone else does, and you might be surprised at your results. Look for ancillary benefits that may go unnoticed by the client or others. If you conduct thorough client interviews, you should uncover many possible areas for extending the value of your offer.

Let's say you are an information systems outsourcer. The obvious sources of value for your services include reduced costs to your clients for systems management, maintenance, and staff. Outsourcing might also reduce the costs of recruiting and retaining employees, as well as professional development programs for some of them. Calculating the value of these savings, though time-consuming, should be a standard exercise for you. So expect your competitors to arrive at similar estimations of value. Take the next step: Use the information you collect to find extensions of that value. See the organization through the client's eyes, and search for less obvious, but important, sources of value that will strengthen your offer.

Maybe you learned through your client interviews, for instance, that the organization was struggling to fund and staff several other initiatives. Instead of proposing, as outsourcers often do, that you hire the client's managers into your firm, perhaps some could stay behind to assist with new initiatives. You could offer training to those managers as a way to grow them into more competent managers who could make an outstanding contribution to new projects.

By uncovering new sources of value, you strengthen your service offer in ways that will be unmatched by your competitors. You should be able to find opportunities for unexpected value by thinking through the logical extensions of your services. Don't settle for the narrow definition buyers give you. Find all possible sources of value and include them in your communications with the client. It will be worth the effort.

Element 4: Mitigation of Risks

As soon as a client gets serious about change, expect a shift in focus to the details of what to do and how to do it. Once that shift occurs, the subject of risk becomes top of mind. And that perception of risk may be your highest hurdle to closing the sale. It isn't enough to offer a case for change; you also have to show that you have fully accounted for the risk of undertaking any initiative and mitigated that risk wherever possible.

Every business problem has its own risk profile, which means that the client may place more emphasis on one element of risk than another. Clients will want to know the answers to a slew of "What happens if . . . ?" questions. Here are some examples:

- What happens if a key member of the team leaves during the project?
- What happens if the early warnings on the budget point to a problem?
- What happens if staffing assumptions turn out to be wrong and we don't have enough people to get the job done?
- What happens if we miss a key deadline?
- What happens if it turns out that your people don't have the right skills?

You'll usually find that clients are most concerned with five broad areas of risk: talent, execution, financial, operational, and career risk. You have to do more than acknowledge those concerns. Be ready to discuss contingency plans to demonstrate how you plan to manage the specific risks of the proposed work. Any of these risks can sink a sale, so be sure you account for all of them.

THE ROOTS OF SERVICE RISK

- *Talent*. Can the proposed people complete the job on time and within budget?
- *Execution*. Is the schedule realistic? Is scope overly ambitious, or is staffing insufficient to deliver value as planned?
- *Financial*. Do the proposed budget and project management approach offer safeguards to ensure that finances will remain under control?
- *Operational*. Will the initiative disrupt the business, and will customer, supplier, or employee relationships suffer?
- *Career*. If the project doesn't work as planned, how will it impact my career?

Talent Risk

Because service sales are often people-intensive, many buyers want assurances, beyond the standard resumes, that the assigned people can get the job done. To determine that, it's common for clients to interview proposed team members. Just as in a job interview, clients test each person's level of skill, temperament, and fit with the culture of the client's company.

In other cases, some sellers allow clients to run simulations to test the people who would be working with them. For example, a buyer who wanted to hire a service provider to facilitate a series of strategic planning sessions asked the seller to arrange an abbreviated meeting to show how the point person would manage the facilitation process and to demonstrate the team's effectiveness in a group setting. The client had the chance to see the team in limited action before making a commitment. This type of offer can be especially helpful for sellers who are new to a client account. By removing doubts about the talent risk, this experience gives the client one less reason to say no. In practice, just offering this as an option speaks to the seller's confidence in the proposed talent, thus reducing the client's perception of risk in this area.

Another simple way to reduce talent risk is to offer direct interviews with previous clients—with their permission, of course. Firsthand reference checks are always a powerful way to reduce a buyer's perception of risk. Using a combination of in-person interviews, reference calls, and sample work sessions will usually eliminate most, if not all, talent risk from the buying equation.

Execution Risk

Even if a buyer thinks your people are terrific, they may still question the feasibility of the work itself. It's natural for them to wonder whether the proposed scope is too broad or the objectives are overly ambitious, making the entire undertaking shaky. Most often, this perception of risk signals a client who is uneasy turning over an important assignment (and responsibility for its outcome) to an outsider. For complex problems, plan to use frequent milestones with specific outcomes, especially early in the initiative, so your client can see measurable progress and get early warning of any trouble.

You can also mitigate the client's perception of this risk by offering site visits and reference calls to companies where your team has worked before. Execution risk is perhaps the most common one that buyers cite when arguing against a sale. Be sure to address this hazard with examples from your similar, past work, especially the results. If you have identified risks that the buyer has not, don't dodge the issue; be forthcoming about those concerns and how you plan to counter them.

Your plan could, for example, include the implementation of a small-scale version of the service as a way to prove the concept before the client commits to the entire program. What's most important, though, is to have an honest dialogue with your clients about this subject so *you* can be sure that you have minimized execution risk. Once you're convinced, you should have little trouble showing clients the logic of your approach and gaining their approval.

Financial Risk

Anyone who's been around the services business for even a short time has heard about the runaway project—a nightmare that comes in late, if at all, and wraps up with a wildly blown budget. With one of these black eyes, people find their careers sidetracked, results unmet, and client relationships at risk. Any initiative can run late, but clients worry most about the one that takes on a life of its own, especially if this has happened to them before.

As with any perceived risk, you won't lessen financial worries with a single tactic. For one, work with clients to construct a fee and expense model that allows for the precise visibility they need. Too often, sellers don't work closely enough with buyers on this issue until it's too late. Once the client has concerns about payment, your cash flow from the account is likely to suffer until you address those concerns.

You can also mitigate risk by tying the payment schedule to the completion of milestones. That way, the client can easily monitor progress and, at the same time, keep tabs on the budget. Take care that you address the client's perception of financial exposure without penalizing your own business, though. Be sure that whatever approach you take on progress payments, you are not going out on a limb by shifting all of the financial risk to you.

The most straightforward way to eliminate financial risk is to propose a fixed fee for the job. No matter how long it takes or what you have to do to finish, the client's exposure is a known quantity. This offers total predictability for the buyer. Be sure to protect yourself, too, by insisting on a reliable method for tracking and resolving scope changes that may impact your overall level of effort. Again, share risk with the client; don't assume it all yourself.

Operational Risk

For many service sales, the resultant organizational changes can be significant, leading to client concerns about disruptions to the business. The source of concern could be potential disruptions to the flow of work, which can impact customer service, supplier delivery, or employee productivity. Anytime an organization finds itself in a state of transition, expect concerns about operational problems.

Most often, operational snafus result from poor communication, inadequate education, lack of an effective backup plan, or some combination of these factors. As you communicate with clients about your service implementation strategy, be sure you can illustrate three important points.

First, demonstrate how you plan to execute a comprehensive communication plan that allows the appropriate individuals to understand what will change, when it will happen, and what they can expect. You will prevent a range of disasters by taking that one step. Second, discuss how you will train the client's staff to work effectively once the proposed change is in place. If people know what they're supposed to do, most will do whatever it takes to make things work. So be sure to show how you will prepare the relevant people to cope with the changes you're proposing.

Finally, always have a contingency plan. Think about the worst-case scenario and plan for its occurrence. If you're proposing to implement a new information system, what would you do if that system failed in its fourth day of operation? Put together a fail-safe plan. You are not likely to need it, but you will ease your client's mind (and help you sleep better) if you have thought it through.

Some disruption to the client's operation is likely during the implementation of most services. But, you can reduce or eliminate operational risks with effective communication, an emphasis on education, and a workable contingency plan.

Career Risk

Whenever you're talking to a client about the impact of a new service on an organization, there's often an unspoken thought rolling around in the client's mind: "If this project doesn't work as advertised, what will it do to me?" Some clients will voice this worry directly. But most times, you won't be sure how important it is. Your best bet is to assume it's at least somewhat important and plan your discussions accordingly.

The source of career concern might be a client's lack of understanding about how you plan to mitigate overall risk for the program. That calls for an open discussion about all the areas of risk, your evaluation of the probability of each occurring, and where the initiative is most vulnerable. You can also explain what steps the client can take to assist the service team with overall risk management.

Addressing client risks assumes, naturally, that you are able to identify them in the first place. Clients will usually tell you what they are worried about, but look for other indicators as you go through the sales process. Maybe the client is concerned about talent risk because of a previous bad experience. Or perhaps the client knows about projects that were just too ambitious. As you conduct interviews and meet with clients, pay particular attention to past experiences, especially the bad ones. That way, you'll know precisely where the hot buttons are, and you can plan accordingly.

Element 5: Trustworthiness *and* Trust

Tom sat across from Pat, his longtime business adviser and a great resource for Tom's many projects over the years. They were talking about Tom's need for a new performance management system. This was going to be a big undertaking, which could easily last months and generate a windfall for the winner. Trouble was that Tom was certain Pat's team wasn't right for this job, although he had no idea who should get the work.

Pat freely acknowledged her team's lack of specific expertise in this area. But predictably, she asked to submit a proposal, even knowing she wasn't likely to win. Tom gave the go-ahead for a proposal. Then the conversation took an interesting turn. Pat reached into a folder and laid a list on the table with contact details for six service providers whom she considered highly qualified to assist with Tom's project. Pat's sources in the organization had clued her in about this project, so she prepared for her meeting with Tom in the only way she knew: She reflected on the client's need and decided that she could be of the most value by helping Tom find the best possible service provider.

Several weeks later, Pat submitted her proposal for the performance management system project. The competition included two service firms on Pat's recommended list. From Tom's perspective, the decision was clear. He trusted Pat and her team, but he had to select a competitor. Pat reported back to her office that they'd lost the sale, but didn't mention that she was the one who (indirectly) recommended the winning competitor. To Pat, this was an integral part of being Tom's adviser.

Pat's story serves as a good reminder of how to build trust in a buying environment. People are understandably more comfortable buying from those they trust, especially for critical purchases. When you think about hiring an accountant or an architect, for example, you evaluate everything you've heard. But before you decide to buy, you ask yourself, "Do I trust this person [or team]?" If you answer that negatively, you're not likely to say yes to the offer.

A buyer's trust takes your business relationship to new levels. Communications are more open and candid, and everyone's guard drops a bit. Buyers tend to share sensitive information more readily with a trusted seller. And misunderstandings are often easier to resolve. But you have to earn that level of trust.

You might think of earning a buyer's trust in two stages, though they might actually happen simultaneously. First, the buyer decides whether you are trustworthy. That means an assessment of your proven expertise in the area of the client's problem, your professional and personal credibility, and your compatibility with the client's people and culture. You must also demonstrate that you will deliberately act in the buyer's interests, as Pat did. Of course, clients understand that you are in business and must also consider your own self-interest. But, even if it's unconscious, they will be looking signs that you'll tip the balance in their favor if you must choose between their interests and your own.

However, a buyer might deem you trustworthy yet still not be ready to move to the second stage, which is to trust you. In an interview in *Management Consulting News*, Professor Andy Wood of West Virginia University explained it this way:

> Trustworthiness is an evaluative judgment about a person, product/service, or firm—or all three. We assess the elements that determine if someone (or an entity) is worthy of trust, and decide whether or not that person meets our standard of trustworthiness.
>
> By contrast, trust is taking action based on that judgment or assessment. When you put a valued resource in the control of someone else, that is trust. Until you take that action, you may judge someone to be trustworthy and still not trust the person with a specific responsibility.[1]

Aim to be trustworthy *and* trusted. To earn buyers' trust, cultivate the attributes that establish "The Foundations of Buyers' Trust."

THE FOUNDATIONS OF BUYERS' TRUST

Expertise: Is the seller a true expert? Is the person competent and qualified? Does the seller have complete knowledge of the product or service offering?

Credibility: Is the person honest and dependable? Can we rely on the salesperson's promises?

Compatibility: Is the seller approachable, likable, reputable, and respectable? Does the person share the same values, and think and act as we would?

Congruence of interests. Do the seller's interests intentionally include our interests? Can we count on the person to act in our best interests?

Based on "Buyers' Trust of the Salesperson," by John Andy Wood, et al.[2]

You may wonder how to develop that level of trust with a buyer, especially without a previous relationship. It may seem difficult, but you can lay the foundations for a trusting relationship during the sales process. For starters, evidence from a study by Professor Wood shows that a seller's expertise has enormous influence not only on establishing trustworthiness, but also on trust itself.[3] Scruffy Stan—you met him in Chapter 2—personifies the persuasiveness of true expertise. With that in mind, you should create opportunities to demonstrate your expertise in ways that complement the sales process.

One way to do that is to address some aspect of the client's problem before the sales process wraps up. Some service providers host tailored executive briefings for their clients to highlight issues the clients are concerned about and to show the seller's depth of expertise. Others facilitate joint client-seller workshops to collaborate on a range of solutions for the client's challenge. Still others customize demonstrations to offer options for solving the problem.

Through the process of proving your expertise, which builds trust, you also let clients see your approach to the relationship. They can then draw their own conclusions about your (good) intentions. Your job is to create those opportunities for the client's evaluation. Buyers may find you trustworthy, but until you show that you are acting in their best interests, they won't necessarily trust you—or buy from you.

As you put together your strategy to land any services sale, think like a buyer, not like a seller. Buyers don't care about closing the sale with you. They care about what their businesses are going to look like when you have done your work and gone. What precise, sustainable value will your clients achieve? They won't settle for even the most confident assertions that you've "been there, done that." They'll want to see a specific, responsive plan for limiting risks. And most of all, they'll ask the all-important question; "Do I trust this person?" Be certain that you've done everything in your power to demonstrate your trustworthiness and your dedication to their interests. Finally, if you've created an airtight case for change, you're likely to get your buyers to take action, and with some luck, choose you to help.

CHAPTER 7

Who Cares about This Sale . . . and Why?

O n the northeast side of the island of Hawaii stands the world's tallest mountain, Mauna Kea. The dormant volcano soars almost 14,000 feet above sea level, and its snow-capped peaks appear to touch the clouds. But visitors to Mauna Kea's slopes experience less than half of the mountain, as another 16,000 feet of its total elevation are below sea level.

For sellers, much of what occurs in client organizations also ripples below the surface. You certainly can't expect clients to inform you of all the internal deliberations about their businesses (or about you and your competitors). You have to accept that you may never know how every client feels about you, your team, or your proposal. But if you are not aware of the people who could impact the decision to hire you, or why they prefer one service provider over another, you should probably start preparing your "Thanks for the great opportunity" speech.

To give yourself the highest probability of winning, you'll want to fill in as many of those knowledge gaps as possible. You may have done all your homework on the issue that an organization wants to address, but you are whistling into the wind if you don't also understand *who* really cares about the issue, and *why* they care.

Why Clients Buy

Questions about who cares and why bring you right back to the buyer perceptions of value that are so central to your sales strategy. When you think about the value your services offer to clients, bottom-line business gains usually spring to mind first. But perceptions of value are more complex and vary greatly, even among individuals with similar goals in the same organization.

When clients decide to buy services, there are reasons—and then there are *reasons* for those decisions. You've probably heard some people categorize buyer motivations as one part rational and two parts emotional, or vice versa. Others label buying motives as professional and personal. Whatever the label, service buyers have more than one set of motivations for their choices. And it's not always obvious what matters the most to each person. You can present the most innovative solution and bring the brightest team, yet still lose the sale because you missed some deal-breaker detail for one or another of the decision makers.

What Are Their Buying Motivations?	
Professional Criteria	**Personal Factors**
Desire for proposed result	Personal career aspirations
Right project approach	Risk avoidance
Well-conceived schedule	Peer approval
Favorable terms and conditions	Ease of working relationship
Demonstrated industry expertise	Desire to keep control
Quality of proposed people/team	Fear of a poor decision
Team's project management skills	Boost industry visibility
Trust in seller's judgment	Professional development
Postcontract support	Build network

Some decision criteria—such as your track record, method of delivery, and the quality of your team—are clearly visible above the surface. If you pay attention, buyers will tell you what those criteria are. Less easy to discern are states of mind about what's most valuable beyond those requirements. Until you understand buyers' complete perception of value, you may misidentify buying motivations. And that almost always results in a sales strategy that hands the sale to a competitor.

Let's say you're offering to assist a client streamline a sales organization. As you progress through your client interviews, you learn that proven expertise with the client's problem, a fixed price, and an eight-week completion schedule top the list of requirements. Some salespeople would jump into writing their proposals with these apparent decision factors as the key points of emphasis.

But how would you alter your proposal if you knew that the client manager for the project was being groomed for a big promotion and the project could be a stepping-stone to that new job? Or what if you knew that one of the decision influencers was interested in building a presence in the company's industry association? Naturally, you would still focus on your areas of strength in discussions and in your sales proposal. But you might also address those other buyer considerations.

To speak to the concerns of the manager hoping for promotion, you might emphasize how your experience and your approach will keep the initiative on track. Or maybe you would suggest ways that the project can boost industry visibility, such as developing a case study on the innovative solution you work on together. You could also offer to connect specific client people with others who might be willing to publish a case study or article, or help arrange a speaking slot for a client at an upcoming industry meeting.

Sanity Check: Don't Hesitate to Ask

Some sellers are perfectly happy jotting down the buyer's rational decision criteria and parroting those back. Remember: Selling is personal, so don't try to *guess* at a buyer's motivations. Chances are good that you'll be wrong and kick yourself later. Engage your buyer on the entire range of motivations. Don't back away from the questions that will lead to a responsive proposal. If buyers are not willing to tell you all the reasons that are driving a sale—or can't articulate them—you'll know soon enough. Just ask and listen.

To win the services sale, you must appreciate the value of your work from the buyers' point of view. Expand your thinking to take in as much of the picture as possible. Once buyers are satisfied that you meet their basic requirements, you should expect them to consider how your offer meshes with their other, more subtle, reasons for picking their favorite. And that assessment could tip the scales.

Assemble a Client Value Profile

For services sales, lots of people could have a hand in the decision, especially for complex initiatives. From the purchasing group to the chief financial officer, you face an array of interests and influences, some of which may conflict. Whether the sale is large or small, you need to learn as much as you can about clients' motivations and what they value in the sale.

For significant sales efforts, assemble a *client value profile,* which offers a systematic way to deepen your understanding of the client's environment, issues, and perceptions. This helps you identify the relevant features of value for each person in the decision process and how you can deliver that value. Whether you do the exercise on the back of a napkin or take a more elaborate approach, you should address five questions:

1. Who do you know in the client's organization, and what are their roles?

2. What level of influence does each person have in the buying decision?

3. How would you characterize your relationship with each person who will either participate in the decision or influence it?

4. Are there additional aspects of value that you can offer to specific individuals to enhance your relationship and improve your odds?

5. What actions should you take to strengthen your positions with key people?

What Is a Client Value Profile?

A client value profile looks objectively at the total picture of your relationships in the buyer's organization so you can create a value-based strategy for strengthening those relationships and winning the sale. Using a tool like this is especially important given that the typical complex sale requires you to persuade four to five people; for some sales, you will have to influence even more people, and research shows that number is increasing.[1]

Each client's profile should be simple, targeted, and based on bringing professional and personal value to the client during the sales process. For each client you profile, identify specific action steps, and then track your activities. This sample profile is for an executive working on a program to redesign her company's approach to purchasing raw materials:

Client contact: Lani R., Executive Vice President, Operations

- 15-year company veteran
- Role in project: Project sponsor
- Role in decision: Decision maker
- Status of relationship: Neutral

- Key concerns
  - Complete work successfully with minimal disruption.
  - Identify potential candidates for promotion during program.
  - Improve communications between manufacturing and distribution functions.
  - Attain a new role in an upcoming reorganization.
- Objective: Convert Lani from neutral to leaning toward your proposal
- Action steps
  - Demonstrate phased implementation approach to minimize downtime.
  - Offer to help align promotion criteria with assignment activities and identify candidates for promotion.
  - Emphasize communication component of your plan.
  - Offer introductions to senior executives in other organizations who hold positions similar to the one she aspires to.

Laying all this out allows you to see individual motivations more clearly, identify ways to deliver more value, decide how to allocate resources to the sales effort, and improve the client relationship. You'll also find it an instructive way to analyze the dynamics and politics of the organization that can affect any sales effort. Use it to highlight strengths and weaknesses in your relationships and to communicate with your team on how each relationship is developing.

Once the sale wraps up, use your results to continue building the client relationship. You can use the tool to keep track of your client relationships, target new opportunities, and develop new relationships.

Who Do You Know?

Start your client value profile with a list of everyone you believe will have any part in the buying decision. For smaller sales, this will be a short list. But for larger ones, you're likely to find decision makers and influencers across the organization. Look first at the composition of the client's selection team. To identify others, check the organization charts you gathered (or created) during your interview process. At this stage, you may not know how buyers will make their decision, but that's fine. The question is, "Who cares about this sale?"

You need to know the roles of all the people on your list, both in the organization and with the proposed sale. For instance, if the director of marketing appears to be a player in the matter, learn as much as possible about that person's expected role in the proposed program. That person may have a direct hand in managing the initiative or may be an adviser to the team. Whatever the case, learn what function each person will fill. If you can also find out people's tenure with the organization, past history of promotions, and any challenges they face, you'll have made a great start.

Next, try to pin down what part each individual will play in the decision to award the sale: decision maker, influencer, no role, or unknown. Pigeonholing people may be difficult, as roles often overlap. You should categorize anyone as a decision maker who has the authority to award the work or sits on a committee or task force that can make the decision. Client task forces are rarely teams of equals. But for simplicity, assume that any member of the task force is a decision maker.

By contrast, influencers are those who can steer the decision one direction or another. Often, influencers are technical evaluators, client managers who may participate in the work after the sale, financial or legal executives who look at the contract and budget, and others the initiative will affect.

Some client people you meet may have no say in the decision but could still have a stake in the outcome. For example, you may have discussed inventory management for the hospital emergency room with the affected nurses. The nurses may have no part in hiring you, but they will contribute to the effort once it gets rolling. So they fall into the category of "no role" in the decision. But you'll be unable to get the work done without them. And they can become a valuable source of information as you develop your proposal, so don't ignore them. If you're not sure how people fit into the decision process, label them as unknown, at least until you learn more.

Sanity Check: Job Titles Don't Tell All

Job titles can be misleading and often don't tell you much about where influence lies. It's quite possible for a 20-year veteran of a company to have less influence over a decision to buy than a fast-tracked newcomer. Take your best shot at assessing influence, and plan accordingly. Be sure not to expend too much energy selling to someone who may have an impressive title but little influence.

Your purpose in categorizing people is not to judge them but to help you decide where you should focus your time and effort as the sales process moves forward. It makes sense to spend more time working with the decision makers and influencers than with others, but be aware how easily a person's role can evolve during a sale. Over time, an influencer can become a key decision maker, and vice versa. New decision makers and influencers can also pop up at any time, upsetting all of your plans. You can learn more about these game changers in the next chapter.

At this stage, your information about the people in the decision-making process will be imperfect. That will be especially true if you're working with a new client or if you haven't had access to many people other than your key contact. Your list of names (or lack of names) tells you what you know and what you still need to find out.

What Do They Think about You?

With the details you have, make a subjective assessment of how you believe each person views your offering, your company, and your people. Keep in mind that this assessment will probably change as you learn more about the organization's environment. Focus on the decision makers first, then influencers, then unknowns. If you have few (or no) relationships within the client's organization, don't be concerned. Size up the challenge you're facing for this specific opportunity. For the people on your list, assign each to one of the following five categories: advocate, leaning toward, neutral, leaning against, or detractor. Scan your completed list to get a sense of your current positioning, and continue your thinking about how to manage the sales opportunity.

WHERE DO THEY STAND?

Think of each person involved in the sales process as one of the following:

Advocate: Actively supports choosing you.

Leaning toward: Shows a preference for your proposal, but may need to see more evidence.

Neutral: Shows no preference for any of the choices.

(continued)

Leaning against: Appears to favor a competitor, but open to learning more.

Detractor: Clearly favors a competitor or not hiring an outsider at all.

Unknown: Individual's preference is uncertain.

With a long list of neutral relationships, you may devote more time to making sure that those clients know who you are and what you (and your team) can do. Your goal is to make an assessment of your relationships to organize your selling process. For example, if you have an influential detractor on your list, decide whether to attempt to salvage the relationship or to try another strategy. Above all, though, don't become complacent if your list has many advocates. It doesn't take much for some people to feel neglected, so take care not to unintentionally slight a supporter.

With a completed list of clients, their roles, and preferences, identify what you believe to be the most important source of value for each person. That includes the benefits of the proposed sale, but it could also extend beyond it. If you are proposing to create a new approach to sales forecasting, for example, the client's vice president of manufacturing may anticipate substantial value from that effort. But consider what other, related sources of value you could find for that person. What are the specific challenges that the executive faces? What other issues could you help with? Perhaps the executive is concerned with how your proposed service will impact suppliers, for instance. Look for even minor snags, and offer a resolution. Finding small, but essential, sources of value makes clients appreciate your ability to spot innovative sources of value for the service you are proposing. And that impression may be enough to win the work.

In one case, a service provider working on a sales opportunity learned that a key decision maker was worried that her staff was unaware of all the business challenges ahead for the company. Though not directly related to subject of the sale, the seller suggested a group meeting and presentation to discuss industry trends and the competitive issues facing the organization, which the client executive agreed to facilitate.

Together, they offered the presentation to 25 people in a one-hour session. Due to its popularity, the seller repeated the session three more times. In the meantime, the seller's proposal was winding its way through the client's decision-making process. The seller won the work, established credentials as an industry expert, and formed several new relationships along the way. All it took was responding to a client concern with a useful solution.

Formulate Your Action Plan

It isn't always easy to know what buyers value, but it's worth trying to figure out. Before you go too far, though, determine which people in the client's organization you should expend energy on. You may decide that those you have categorized as detractors aren't going to change their minds, so you might not try to win them over. Or you may believe that two of the people you think are neutral could make the difference in the decision. Plan to spend more time determining how you can add value to your sales process for them.

Look beyond the people you have categorized as advocates. Resist the natural tendency to gravitate toward the people who like you and support your efforts. Decide how you can help those you believe are neutral, unknown, and even detractors. Your goal is to keep your existing supporters on your side, but also to create new ones.

You might ask an advocate to talk to those who are leaning toward or are neutral about the value of your services, for example. On the other hand, if a supporter's bias is too obvious within the buyer's organization, it might be better for you to work directly with someone who is still on the fence. And be sure you haven't incorrectly characterized anyone before you take any action. Assuming neutrality for someone who is actually a detractor can have disastrous consequences.

To complete the client value profile, plan the specific steps to take with each individual to move your sales effort ahead. Develop the actions, responsibilities, expected results, and due date for the steps you identify. If you know that one of your client executives wants to know how other companies handle a specific type of customer account, assign someone to gather and communicate that information to the client. If you have clients on your list you'd like to work with, but don't know what they value, your first task is to ask them. You may schedule a short meeting to discuss the project and probe the client's key points of interest. Offer assistance, if you think it makes sense and moves the sale forward.

As part of this final step, you'll learn more about why each person cares about the sale, and that information will be invaluable to your ongoing sales effort. Once you have discovered all the sources of client value, make sure those findings make their way into your presentations and sales proposal; otherwise, you risk the client labeling you as one of those service providers who doesn't listen.

As discussed in Chapter 6, every services sale has five components: a compelling story, a case for change, a clear expression of value, a plan for minimizing risk, and mutual trust. As you pursue a sale, developing a comprehensive view of value is one of your greatest challenges. Understanding who really cares about the sale, and why, is essential to meeting that challenge. Your understanding of buyers' motivations will help you adapt to the shifts that invariably happen during the sales cycle.

CHAPTER 8

Shift Happens: Predicting Surprises

The future is bound to surprise us, but we don't have to be dumbfounded.

—Kenneth Boulding[1]

When he was a boy, Mordecai "Three Finger" Brown lost two fingers on his throwing hand, yet still became one of the dominant baseball pitchers of all time. He threw 55 career shutouts and helped the Chicago Cubs win four pennants and two World Series titles between 1906 and 1910. Brown's secret weapon was his devastating curveball, which left batters totally bewildered.[2] Studies in physics show that a curveball like Brown's deviates only 3.4 inches from a straight line drawn from the pitcher's hand to the catcher's glove. But, from the batter's perspective, the ball appears to "break" more than 14 inches from that straight line.[3]

As the curveball attests, perceptions have a huge impact on performance. Great hitters say you can change all that, though, if you know that a curveball is coming. Those hitters work on their skills to spot a curveball, anticipate its flight, and improve their odds of connecting with it.

Five Predictable Surprises

If you sell services, you know that curveballs come with the territory. The selling process can be perplexing and rife with personalities and politics. You may never be certain whom you are competing against—or whether you're in the running at all. If you ask sellers why they lost out, you often hear that the client pulled the rug out from under them near the end of the sales process. Maybe the surprise was a change in scope or a case of cold feet about the price. Whatever the curveball, something is bound to mess with your plans before the end of the sale.

Some surprises do come out of the blue, such as a buyer canceling the effort at the last minute. But many other so-called surprises are predictable—for instance, a change in direction in the middle of the sale. Most surprises shouldn't throw you for long, especially if you remain in close contact with your buyer. Instead of responding to a surprise with alarm (or dread), view it as a signal to alter the way you are selling. That often means changing the way you express your offer's value to the buyer.

Changes in clients' buying processes, especially in midsale, often reflect their evolving knowledge about you, your service offer, and how you propose to implement the service. As clients learn more about the details of your offer, that adds to *their* expertise on the matter, which alters their evaluation of your service. And, as clients get into those details, it's natural for them to draw others into the planning and into the sales process. It's also common for clients to search for alternatives if they perceive gaps in your offer. The result of that assessment usually means you'll see another competitor on the scene.

Thinking like a buyer means that you continuously ask yourself what steps *you* would take to make the right buying decision; if you do that, you'll find that most surprises are predictable. You can anticipate and be ready to manage the implication of surprises—before they happen. Of course, you'll be able to predict the next curveball only if you're plugged into what the client is doing and thinking about the sale. So, rule number one for managing surprises is to always keep an open line of communication with the decision makers. And, whenever possible, take each surprise in stride and avoid scrambling to answer every new question the buyer brings up.

Sanity Check: Some Surprises Are Good for You

When an unexpected event occurs during a sale—especially the arrival of a new competitor—you might fear the worst. It's common to react to such news with an assumption that your proposal is floundering, so the buyers are looking elsewhere. That could be the case, but there are other, positive ways to interpret their action. Maybe they have chosen you, but they want a comparative bid. Perhaps one of them is doing a favor for a colleague by looking at another proposal. Don't jump to conclusions when clients surprise you. It's entirely possible that your initial take on the matter is off base. Instead, keep your perspective, ask questions, and then decide how to respond.

You'll find that five predictable surprises crop up in most selling processes, so be sure your sales plan accommodates each of these:

1. Slow communication
2. Change in project direction
3. More emphasis on price
4. Introduction of new decision makers
5. Entry of a new competitor

Slow Communication

The first surprise can crop up after even one sales call. You've just finished a great meeting, and the client seems enthusiastic about working together. You listened well to the issue, started building trust, and engaged in an insight-based dialogue. The client was receptive to your ideas, and the rapport was so good that you agreed to write a proposal after a single meeting.

You let people at your office know about the opportunity and then get busy with the research for your proposal. But when you send an e-mail to the client for clarification on a point, it takes a few days to hear back. You eventually receive a cryptic response suggesting a meeting in the next 10 days or so. You are surprised and discouraged.

No matter how well your first meeting goes, make no assumptions about your prospects. Maybe you do have the job wrapped up; you can find lots of cases where that happens. But initial meetings are fact-finding missions for buyers, so don't expect the red-carpet treatment every time you call. Clients may be sincere about wanting to work with you, but they may also be talking to others. More often than not, early meetings *are* positive, because everyone is on their best behavior, so that may not be a signal one way or the other.

Keep your attention on whether you want to work with this client. Complete your qualification process with due diligence so that, when the client does call, you're ready to roll. Lack of communication early on should not take you by surprise, and you shouldn't read anything more into it than warranted.

Change in Project Direction

When you coinvent your services with buyers, the process is an evolutionary one. As they discover more about what they really need and what you can do, there will be shifts in the overall design of the service. Changes in direction may impact one or more aspects of your service, but it's common for clients to make changes in the proposed approach, in the scope of the effort, or both. Because these factors are so closely inter-related, a change to one usually impacts the other. For example, if your client wants to increase the scope of the proposed program from one region to two regions, your approach to the work will also change. If your client wants to reduce the price, you may suggest scaling back the scope or modifying the approach to the work.

Changes in direction often emerge as clients get serious about making a commitment to move ahead. As a sale approaches a decision, watch for growing involvement in the process by new decision influencers. While you are promoting your service, your key contacts are also selling the service—to others in *their* organizations. As the service offer takes shape, expect buyers to broaden the team of people who participate in the process. These new people can include those the decision makers look to for guidance and those who must agree with or approve the sale. As your buyer seeks out the opinions and approval of others, expect changes in the direction of buyer's thinking—and your proposal.

Your competitors are also forces for changes in the client's direction. They'll offer their own opinions on how to manage scope, approach, and costs to secure the most benefit from the effort. If the client embraces those opinions, they will eventually alter how the client wants to proceed. Pinpointing the source does not matter nearly as much as understanding the nature of the change and amending your sales strategy when necessary.

Revising Project Approach

Changes in direction often mean you have to revisit your proposed approach to the assignment. Your buyers could ask for an earlier comple-tion date than you'd originally planned, or maybe they want you to organize the effort in a different way than you intended.

When you face a change in approach, take two actions immediately. The first is to validate the assumptions behind your proposal. For example, if the client wants you to deliver the service sooner, examine how that impacts the size of your team and your fee. If you get this wrong, even by a small amount, your profit could evaporate.

Second, go back through your proposed timeline to ensure that you can achieve the clients' new schedule. Examine how the compressed schedule impacts your ability to get the right resources (especially people) when you need them. And be certain that the clients can meet their commitments with the tighter schedule. You may believe that you can complete the work in the revised time frame, but the clients must also do their part for you to finish on time.

Never agree to changes in approach, especially to the schedule, before you do your homework. You may believe you know enough about the sale to make a reasoned judgment without getting bogged down in a detailed analysis. That may be true, but you could also end up making the common mistake of overpromising, and then underdelivering. If that happens, you may do irreparable damage to the client relationship. When clients ask you to change the schedule, especially for a complex sale, don't hesitate to request time to study the ramifications before responding. By doing that, you'll protect your own interests, and your client will appreciate your thorough treatment of this important aspect.

Managing a Slippery Scope

When Jeanne came out of the meeting with her client sponsor, Ryan, she was kicking herself. Her team had written a comprehensive sales proposal, and now Ryan was telling her that they needed to "scale back the program a bit." Not only was Ryan running into resistance about going forward with the initiative, but his colleagues were griping that the proposed fee seemed out of line with the expected value. Jeanne was upset, because she had known that this scenario was a possibility but had put the concern aside; she should have discussed it with the client before she and her team finished and delivered their proposal.

Ryan suggested that they brainstorm about how to reduce the scope of the effort and the fee while retaining as much value as possible. Jeanne got to work with the client, knowing that a major rewrite of her proposal awaited her and the sales team.

Changes in scope aren't inevitable, but they are common. Try to anticipate them as early as possible in the sales process. In your initial sales conversations, introduce the subject of scope. Try to narrow down, for example, the precise parts of the organization you'll work with and the people who will participate. Talk to clients about options, test different scenarios, and settle on your statement of scope. This can be difficult to accomplish, but the more clarity you achieve, the easier it will be to manage subsequent changes.

Then, keep a running dialogue with clients about the limits of what you plan to do, especially what you are *not* including. Return often to your estimate of the schedule, fee, and approach. Be sure clients are comfortable with all the implications of the original definition of scope. Last, be ready with new scenarios that reflect how you would undertake the work with alternative boundaries. No need to create written estimates that you can hand over on the spot, but do the legwork on the possibilities ahead of time so you can respond confidently if a buyer asks, "What would happen if we did this at all three call centers instead of just one?"

How you define and manage proposed scope during the sale can reduce the shock if the client wants a revamp. What's more, if you are precise about scope during the sale, your implementation efforts will go more smoothly. Too many projects and relationships are derailed by preventable misunderstandings about what buyers thought sellers promised to do. So make a continuous effort to get and keep a workable, though flexible, definition of scope.

Stay on top of the clues you get from clients that a change in scope is in the offing. Ask questions that test the client's comfort level with the scope and approach before you commit everything to a proposal. That attention will reduce the need for substantial changes later, and it will help keep the rest of your sales process on track.

Be the Force for Change

The best way to manage many of the inevitable surprises in the sales process is for *you* to be the source of the shifts. After all, you lead the definition of your service, its scope, approach, and implementation. As the sale progresses, you are in a unique position to find new ways to view the problem and to deliver your services faster, more easily, or with less disruption. As you refine your thinking, bring your client along on these improvements to your offer. Some shifts in the sales process should come from you, not the client or your competitors.

More Emphasis on Price

In early meetings with buyers, you often hear that price isn't their driving concern. Finding the right service provider to do the best job possible trumps price, they say. At the outset, this perspective makes sense. But as the sale draws to a close, price will begin to dominate the discussion. Of course, buyers have price on their minds to some extent all along. For some, like public-sector clients, price has to be the primary selection criterion. But you can safely assume that most buyers want to find the right people for the job before addressing the issue of price.

Once buyers are convinced they have found the right experts, their priorities frequently shift to an evaluation of price. They focus on payment terms, conditions, expenses, and the language of the proposed contract or engagement letter. This increased emphasis on price shouldn't surprise you. You can usually see this renewed interest in price as an indicator that your client has, so far, been satisfied.

At that point in the sales process, some buyers will ask for concessions, such as lower fees or no up-front payments. Naturally, buyers hope to get the best deal possible. Assuming that you price your services in alignment with the value you are proposing to deliver, this conversation should be straightforward. Chapter 11 covers negotiating for a range of pricing strategies in more detail, but the point is always to connect the perceived value of your solution to your proposed fee. And show the relationship between the scope of the project, the expected value, and the proposed fee. Once you establish those connections, you can illustrate the ways in which you can change the fee.

If you are meeting with buyers about your fee, steer the conversation to alternatives. Instead of showing a single price, offer choices. Show more than one scenario for scope and fees. Vary assumptions for staffing, the schedule, and who will take on particular tasks. For each option, present a rationale for the fee and an estimate of expected value. Offering options probably won't deter some clients from asking for a lower fee or more generous terms, but it demonstrates your flexibility and willingness to compromise.

Some sellers worry that any price negotiation can jeopardize a client relationship. Sometimes, wrangling over fees does get tough. You must decide what is more important, a client relationship or a profitable business. Naturally, having both is preferable and possible. But once you give up your profit in a price negotiation, you're not likely to get it back. And most low-profit assignments don't go as well as planned. Be mindful of the impact of all price concessions.

Introduction of New Decision Makers

Any shift in a client's decision-making team can be unnerving. If you must suddenly work with new (and often unknown) people, your first thought might be that they will undo all your hard work simply because they don't know you.

Chris, a seller of project management services to retail organizations, faced such a situation. It all started with a brief e-mail informing him of a room change for an upcoming sales meeting. Chris and his team had planned the meeting down to the last detail, including how they would split up the presentation and how they would engage each of the seven client managers that they confirmed would be attending the meeting. The team arrived for the meeting early and gazed around the echoing conference room, wondering if they had misunderstood the e-mail. But no—as they set up, their client sponsor arrived with the news that the meeting would now include 14 people rather than the 7 originally planned. Many of the newcomers, their sponsor explained, had a hand in approving the final list of sellers, but had not actively participated in the process before. Chris had to devise plan B for the meeting on the fly.

The introduction of new decision makers (or influencers) is one of the more predictable surprises in selling services. Nobody likes being blind-sided like Chris's team was, and anytime a new decision maker appears, it can make you start pulling out your hair. Instead, your response should be to dispassionately determine the impact on the sale. Sometimes, new decision makers bring welcome change; other times, their addition is neutral. Whatever the case, assess how the change affects you and adapt your strategy accordingly.

To do that, update your client value profile with the newest players in the sale. As you did previously, identify each person's role, tenure with the organization, key challenges, and relationships within the company. Assess your relationships with the new decision makers and draw up a series of potential actions to help you learn more about these people. This exercise will give you a good sense of how to change your approach to the sale.

When new decision makers enter the sales process toward the end, it's up to you to make sure they understand what your team brings to the table. Don't expect that the newcomers will automatically trust your credentials, even if others in the organization think you walk on water. Look for opportunities to brief any new decision makers on the details of your proposal instead of relying on others to speak on your behalf. You may not get the chance, but you must try. If you do meet with a new decision maker, particularly someone you haven't met before, don't start the discussion with a recitation of your credentials. Begin with what matters most: your understanding of the problem, expected value, and organizational impact.

You may not get *any* advance warning from clients about new decision makers, so always be ready for this curveball. To help you find out everyone who might participate in the sale, don't be shy about asking buyers "Who else?" questions, such as the following:

- Who else do you think we should talk to?
- Who else will review our sales proposal?
- Who else will be involved in your reference calls?
- Who else will attend our presentation?
- Who else will be on the selection team?
- Who else will help you make the decision?

Like many surprises in the sales process, it's difficult to know whether a change in the group of decision makers is good or bad for your sale. But try to anticipate *when* it might happen, *who* might join the team, and *how* to respond.

Entry of a New Competitor

Once a sales process is under way, you're probably not going to think it bodes well for your chances if the buyer invites a new competitor to bid on the work. The entry of a new competitor usually creates a mad scramble among the other sellers as they try to figure out what it means. A new competitor may turn up after the emergence of one or more new decision makers, who may want to bring in their preferred service providers. Or maybe they believe that the selection committee is overlooking a qualified choice. It's also possible that the buyers want a broader set of ideas. Or perhaps they think the sellers they're seeing just aren't going to cut it.

You may not know the reason, especially at first. Keep your eyes and ears open to work out how the decision process and your role may change. Remember, competitors are often the source of changes in direction, so don't be surprised when such changes occur shortly after the entry of a new rival. Don't put your effort on hold; continue to execute your plan. You want to know as much as possible, of course. But you can control only your own proposal and its projected value, not what competitors are doing. A new competitor shouldn't be cause for serious alarm unless you're not bringing buyers the value they expect. And that won't be a secret. You'll know.

Like so many of the challenges you face in selling, communication is key in predicting surprises. Follow three simple steps and you won't be blindsided by change. First, stay in frequent contact with clients during the sale. Assume that things will change, and ask permission to check in to help them track and manage those changes. Most clients will readily agree. Next, always conduct interim reviews of your developing sales proposal with your buyers. Some sellers have minimal communication with clients while drafting their proposals, preferring to hold off with a review until they have an acceptable draft. If you follow this approach, you will almost surely find later that something changed since you began working on your proposal.

Finally, keep your mind open for new ways to approach the client's issue and recommend those changes to your client. As you work out the details of any proposal, you find nuances that can modify the scope or approach of the assignment. You may uncover a faster method using fewer resources. Share those options with your client before you finish your proposal. Not only will you have a way to test your own new ideas, but you'll also stay current on any changes the client wants to make.

The best way to manage a perceived threat to your sale is to convert it to your advantage. Stay a step ahead by anticipating potential shifts and how you can approach such changes. Stick with bringing value to the client throughout the sales process, and you'll find some way to make every surprise, predictable or not, an opportunity to win.

CHAPTER 9

The Perfect Sales Proposal

Nothing happens until someone sells something.

—Thomas Watson Sr., IBM[1]

After Thomas Watson uttered that simple declaration to IBM staffers two generations ago, it morphed into a standard rallying cry to motivate legions of salespeople everywhere to get out there and sell something. What's missing from Watson's mantra is that, these days, few businesses sell anything, at least to other businesses, without a sales proposal.

Every three months in the United States alone, businesses that use some kind of proposals for selling generate more than $250 billion in sales.[2] Given that many buyers solicit multiple proposals for each sale, proposal writers and sales professionals could be the busiest people in business. At any given moment, thousands of sellers are writing or presenting proposals to buyers. The trouble that plagues most of them is that the underlying value of the seller's offer doesn't shine through, and so the sales process devolves into profit-busting haggling over price.

For example, imagine you are Toni, a client executive, as she rolls over to a stack of sales proposals sitting on the edge of her desk. She reaches first for the one from the favored provider and leafs through it quickly to get a sense of how long it might take to read. She dives in. The executive summary begins, "We are pleased to present this proposal to Stellar Industries. We understand that Stellar wants to conduct a company-wide review of the effectiveness of its production planning process, and we believe that we are uniquely qualified to undertake that review." The summary continues in that vein, with platitudes and assertions of superiority that have Toni shaking her head. She tosses the proposal to the side and gets on the phone to make some pressing calls that she thought of as she read the proposal.

If the seller only knew what happened. That proposal, which should have rallied Toni to support the sale, had the opposite effect. Before she finished reading the executive summary, the seller had lost a precious opportunity to influence her decision.

Sadly, many proposals suffer the same fate. That's significant, because no matter how well you manage your sales process, there's a 99.9 percent chance that you'll write some sort of a proposal to seal the deal. Whether your buyer wants a one-page engagement letter or a multivolume response to an RFP, the challenge is the same: You must put together a proposal that tells a compelling story, reinforces the buyer's trust in you, *and* makes it obvious that you are the right choice.

Given that you have to create most sales proposals quickly, meeting that challenge is anything but simple. With few exceptions, by the time most buyers are ready to seek outside help, they usually want to get moving yesterday. The buyer's sense of urgency means that you have to scramble to get your offer ready. Too often, the resulting proposal looks impressive on the surface, with colorful fonts and bold graphics, but disappoints with lifeless content, pieced together from the fragments of other documents. What's worse is when the seller's self-promotion drowns out the key reasons the buyer is seeking outside help to begin with.

Speed is essential, and many sellers accelerate the proposal process by writing about what they know best—themselves. When a deadline looms, it's tempting to emphasize, in a generic way, how well qualified you are to meet the client's needs and to spend less time discussing the client's issue. However, once you sacrifice insight for speed, your proposal looks just like every other one your client will receive.

Even a perfect proposal won't close a sale by itself. But a generic one that is plagued with self-serving (and boring) language can quickly upend an otherwise flawless sales process, as well it should.

It isn't difficult to make your proposal more about the client and less about you. Begin by looking at how often you start a sentence with *we*, because what follows is probably about your qualifications or your company's guiding principles. Except in the section that's specifically about your company, remove the self-congratulations from your proposal. Remember, buyers have very little interest in your organization—except how it can help them run their businesses.

Scratch These Losers from Your Proposals	
Eliminate:	**Because:**
We are pleased	They already know this.
We understand (or believe)	Discuss what you *know* about the issues.
Our highest priority is your satisfaction	This claim is self-serving and dubious.
We are committed	Your commitment is a given.
We focus on quality	Your clients will hope this is the case.
We value	Tell clients what they can expect from you.
We are uniquely qualified	It's rare that only one seller is qualified.
We are the premier providers	You should not be the one to say this.
We offer a comprehensive solution	As opposed to what?
We put the customer first	This cliché offers nothing useful to your client.
We are the right choice	The client makes this decision.

Communicate your knowledge of those concerns, and what you bring, by taking three steps in your proposal. First, stick to the issues in the proposal summary. Emphasize the clients' challenge, how it will impact their future, and the imperative for making a change. You'll get more selling power from a clear rendering of your understanding of the challenge than you will from claims that you are uniquely qualified.

Second, keep the proposal as short as possible. Resist the urge to load it up with meaningless graphics and images. Get the facts and the substance of your approach down, in a concise manner, without fussing over glitz. Finally, examine every page, paragraph, and sentence in your proposal. Who is the subject of each sentence? Is it you, or is it your clients? In every instance possible, make sure you are talking about them. Save your sales hype for the section of your proposal where everyone does need to see it— your qualifications.

Who Will Read *Your* Proposal?

In addition to the language, you can boost the impact of a sales proposal another way: Write your proposal with specific people firmly in mind.

Though it's a handy construct we all use, the generic "client" does not really exist. In his book, *On Writing*, author Stephen King tells us that unless you write directly to someone (he calls that person his Constant Reader), " . . . you are just a voice quacking in the wind."[3] Failing to zero in on a reader is a real danger for sales proposals because of the variety of people who end up reading them, including technical evaluators, procurement executives, department heads, and others. Anticipating a mix of interest from such a diverse group of readers can lead you to write to none of them.

Which readers should you write your proposal to? If it's a small business with only one decision maker, your audience is obvious. If it's not so clearcut, before you begin writing, ask your client who will review the proposal and in what order. Then, focus on the expectations of those who will have the greatest influence on the fate of your proposal: the first and last readers.

In competitive sales, the first reader is often an evaluator or recommender, not a final decision maker. The initial evaluations of proposals usually result in the creation of two piles—"Maybe" and "No." If you don't satisfy the first reader, you don't have a chance. To your first reader, compliance with the stated requirements for the proposal may be as important as other content. Often, the first reader is a veteran of reading proposals, knows every trick in the book, and gets little or no satisfaction from slogging through another round of proposals. Brighten this reader's day by removing any doubt that your proposal matches the client's requirements. Especially for long proposals, you might want to include a simple reference guide illustrating how each section of your proposal corresponds to those requirements.

The point is that without a fast and easy way for your first reader to check compliance, the substance of your proposal will get a less thorough review, and it is much more likely to end up in the dreaded "No" pile. It's certainly possible that your first reader will be both an evaluator and a decision maker. That simplifies things somewhat, but you still need to shift mental gears to include the latter perspective.

It's not enough to convince yourself that you've covered all the bases in a proposal. The last reader—the decision maker—must agree with you. The last reader often looks at proposals only from the finalists, so the seller's qualifications are rarely in doubt. This reader may focus primarily on your summary or overview, looking for a distillation of your superior understanding of the client's issues, an insightful approach to meeting the desired goals, and extraordinary people to work with.

Look at your past proposals and ask yourself: Was I writing to specific readers? What were their respective roles and expectations? Was the proposal responsive to them? By the way, you will find that, if you write every proposal to the first and last readers, you will also take care of everyone in between.

Sales proposals don't have to be page-turners, but they also shouldn't read like mortgage lending documents. If you fail to engage your key readers with the content, they're likely to assess your proposal solely on price. Once you're battling on price, the most likely casualty is your profit.

Sanity Check: Give Them a Stake in the Proposal

What is the easiest way to make sure that your buyers will read your proposal? Use them as sounding boards for proposal ideas and wording. Give them a stake in the proposal by going over essential components of the proposal with them *before* you submit it. By engaging your buyers in the creation of your proposal, you simplify their eventual review of it and ensure that they will want to check it out thoroughly.

Anchor Your Proposal with *Buyer* Win Themes

Writing with specific readers in mind provides a context for your proposal's content. But you still must fashion targeted content that sells. And that's where many proposals fall short. When sales teams begin to brainstorm about what will go into a proposal, one of the first questions is bound to be, "What do we need to do to win this sale?" This predictable question leads to the exercise of crafting so-called win themes—the reasons why you are the best choice for the job.

The themes usually include standard points such as your long track record of similar assignments, your commitment to get the job done on time and on budget, and your innovative approach for managing the work. The idea is that you then sprinkle these gems throughout your proposal and in subsequent presentations to buyers. These are strong selling points; but the trouble, of course, is that themes about the depth of your experience and the tools you employ are about you, not the buyer.

Why should buyers care what it will take for you to win? They don't. Instead, they ask themselves if the proposal addresses what it will take for *them* to win. In searching for that answer, buyers look for evidence of your ability to deliver the value they need. Once they're convinced that you can do that, they'll look to the other reasons to hire you: your approach, tools, and timeline. If the win theme of your proposal is you, your offer *should* wind up on the "No" pile. Naturally, buyers know that your promotional pitch is coming. But, as with the rest of your client communication, that pitch should not be the first or most obvious thing vying for their attention in your proposal.

You can transform a seller-focused proposal into a buyer-focused one by flipping the questions you ask yourself at the beginning of the proposal creation process. Instead of trying to figure out what it will take for you to win, ask what it will take for the client to win. This slight change in your thinking often uncovers essential points you can address to create a powerfully differentiated proposal.

For example, if you learn about a planned organizational shake-up in your client's area of responsibility, you might emphasize your team's skills in managing initiatives in the midst of disruptive internal changes. You could also demonstrate how your proposal mitigates the risk of such change. If you know that your project will be one of many that your client sponsor will have to juggle, you can point out how you help clients work through resource constraints when people have competing demands on their time.

A buyer win theme is not about why you are better than your competitors. Don't even imply that the reason you should win is that someone else should not. It's never a good idea to bet your success on the failings or mistakes of others. In fact, your win theme should not pit you against the competition at all, but against the client problem or need you're trying to address. It communicates that you listened to—and heard—everything the client said and that you have tailored a solution to meet the client's goals. Your win theme is not a recitation of your track record with other clients. It is a series of specific, relevant, understandable, compelling, and workable ideas on what it will take for your clients to have exceptional success if they hire you.

Think of the buyer-focused win theme as the central part of the story you're building to communicate how you'll help the client. You should have been validating your thinking about the relevance and impact of this message with the client throughout the sales process. And it's critical to nail it in your proposal. Buyer win themes aren't always obvious. Analyze all your interview notes and think through your impressions to come up with a set of buyer win themes that will set you apart from others.

What you learned during client interviews and sales meetings is the raw material for crafting a buyer win theme. That's another reason why the quality of your interview process is so essential to your success. If you've asked the right questions, listened intently to the answers, and assimilated the information effectively, you can create buyer win themes that are relevant to the client and support your effort to close the sale. Buyer win themes, by themselves, aren't enough to win a sale, but you'll use them to prepare the most important part of your sales proposal, the case for change.

Anatomy of a Sales Proposal

Once you have your buyer win themes, your task is to organize those ideas into your written sales proposal. What other content should you include in your proposal? If you answer five questions in your proposal, you'll have a head start over most of your competitors. By now, these questions should sound familiar:

1. Do you really understand the problem and the case for change?
2. Do you have a compelling vision for the future?
3. Is there significant value above the cost?
4. Is your team a good fit?
5. Can you really do what you claim?

The core of any successful sales proposal is an indisputable case for the proposed change and for you to be the one to help make that change a reality. Chapter 6 covered this imperative; now you need to communicate it in your proposal by writing about the need for the change, the expected value, and the vision for the future. If you don't convince your proposal readers on these three points, it won't matter how good your services are, because clients won't buy from you.

Divide your proposal into seven sections: (1) a summary, (2) the need for change, (3) scope and strategy, (4) expected results, (5) people/team, (6) timing and fees, and (7) your qualifications. You may find that your proposal warrants separating one or more of these combined sections. In some proposals, for example, you may want to separate scope from strategy, or timing from fees. Organize your proposal according to the buyer's needs. Just be sure you cover each of these subjects in any sales proposal.

What Every Sales Proposal Should Include	
Proposal summary	A short, stand-alone section that reinforces the case for change and outlines the clients' future.
The need for change	Why does the client need to make a change?
Scope and strategy	How will you achieve the desired results?
Expected results	What is the quantified value or impact of your offer?
People/team	Who will deliver the results?
Timing and fees	How long will it take? How much will it cost?
Qualifications	Why choose you?

The Need for Change

Let's save the discussion of the proposal summary for last and focus first on the case for change, which always rests on the client's issue, its implications, and what the client will achieve by agreeing to your proposal. Your goal is to outline the background and the objectives of the initiative. If productivity in your client's call center is slumping, for example, discuss the impact of that slump on revenue, customer service, employee retention, and costs. If you've done a good job with your client interviews, you should have all the facts you need to back up your assertions of the implications.

Use facts to prove the need for change, but resist overwhelming proposal readers with data. Instead, frame your argument with as much qualitative information as quantitative data. As discussed in Chapter 6, you'll make a more forceful impression on decision makers if you tell the story behind the numbers. Just make sure you answer the question: Do you really understand the problem and the case for change?

From there, portray what you see for the client's future once you complete your work. Specifically, what will change for your clients once they accept your proposal and you do what you promised? Buyers need that well-reasoned vision for what they can expect in the future. The more details you can offer, the easier it will be for them to evaluate your proposal. You may choose to express the future using quantitative data, such as improved financial or operational performance, or qualitative gains, but your vision must be believable.

Most readers will look at a sales proposal with a jaundiced eye, and they'll test whether they really believe your view of the future. Pass that test and you're bound to move on in the sales process. Flunk it and you will probably lose the sale to a stronger competitor.

Scope and Strategy

After you make it clear that you grasp the need for change and have a vision for the future, move on to how you intend to assist the client in reaching the end state. Use this section to define the boundaries or scope of the project and the strategy for achieving the objectives. Specify precisely where and with whom you will work. For instance, your effort might be limited to the Midwest region, or to one company division, department, or group of people.

You'll also outline your strategy or approach for completing the work. Use this section to discuss how you'll organize to do the work, including what tasks you and others will perform, how you will form the team(s), how you plan to integrate and manage the teams, and what tools you'll use. Some clients won't care what methods you employ; others will be keenly interested. More than one client has asked to review every detail of a service provider's methodology. Be sure to ask about this before you write your proposal. If they do want to know about your tools, tailor the explanation to the level of detail they want. If that's a lot of text, consider summarizing it in this section and creating a separate appendix for the details.

Those who read this section must be able to make a direct connection between the approach you propose and the achievement of the end state. Without that direct connection, expect the client to either reject your proposal outright or send you back for a rewrite. Before you deliver your proposal, examine your plan from the client's perspective. Can you see how the approach you've described will lead to the end state? If you cannot, look for ways to revise your proposal so that connection between objectives and approach stands out.

Expected Results

You may discuss the client's expected results in the summary, objectives, and service fee sections. Even so, you should have a separate section that answers the client question, "What *exactly* are we getting?" Some sellers call this section *deliverables* or *outcomes* instead of expected results. The description of results usually receives special scrutiny because it specifies what clients will get for their money. To pass muster, the results section must be unambiguous in its depiction of what the client can expect.

If you claim, for instance, that your service will improve an organization's ability to manage deployment of workers to specific jobs, you may get a lot of questions from the client about the quantitative impact of that change. If, however, you say that your service will improve labor deployment while reducing salary costs by 4 percent and overtime expenses by 9 percent, the value of your result is clear and therefore subject to fewer questions about what the client stands to gain.

By offering precision in your results statement, you also aid the people who will deliver those results. They will know exactly what it will take to achieve success. They'll have a definite goal to work toward. And the clients will have a clear benchmark for assessing their overall satisfaction with your service.

People/Team

You probably remember the childhood playground ritual of choosing sides for kickball, dodgeball, or any other game. Two captains would stand before a line of kids and take turns selecting the ones they wanted until everyone was on a team. The scrawny kid who loved math and wasn't very good at sports was always the last one picked.

Team selection in business settings isn't quite so brutal, but few things impact the outcome of any assignment more than the quality of your team. Most sellers know how to choose a service delivery team, but in many cases, you may also have clients on your team. It's particularly important that you select client team members with care (assuming you have a choice), because their contributions can mean the difference between a great outcome and a flameout. It can be difficult to achieve the results you intend if the client has chosen a team before you've had a chance to put in your two cents. Whenever possible, make your preferences known. Here are few quick ideas for picking a productive group.

Put aside your initial visceral responses, and formulate a skills' requirement summary for each role on the team. Then use that summary to narrow down the candidates. But skills aren't everything. With the client's help, assess each person's capacity to work collaboratively with others, especially outsiders; to be creative in ambiguous situations; and to commit to the proposed outcome, even if that means contributing beyond the normal job duties every now and then.

The final test is for that intangible quality—chemistry. You'll know that only when you see or feel it. Reengage your instincts and pay attention to them. The best people are usually busy on other projects. You may have to push to identify the A players and get them on your team. If it's uncomfortable to push, imagine how you'll feel if you don't achieve your goals because of a poorly performing team. You'll put your relationships, reputation, and profit on the line.

And remember, looks don't count. That scrawny math whiz who, years ago, was the last one the team captain picked may be just the person you're looking for.

Timing and Fees

Think about the last time *you* read a sales proposal or a quote for services. What was the first thing you looked at? If you answered the fee section, you're not alone. The section on price will be the most widely read part of your proposal. *Everyone* looks at the price.

Multiple methods are available to calculate price—fixed fee, value pricing, performance-based pricing, or an hourly rate. What matters most is that your fee is defensible. Whenever possible, juxtapose your fee with the anticipated value of your services. For instance, if you propose to deliver $700,000 in cost reduction to your client for a fee of $120,000, make sure your client sees that relationship clearly.

When you choose to attribute a quantified value to the delivery of your service, be conservative. Consider expressing that value in a range instead of using a specific number. Your clients will read your pricing section very carefully and scrutinize all your calculations. On more than one occasion, a seller has lost because the client fixated on the method of that calculation rather than on the substance of the proposal. Be sure that your expression of value is conservative, easy to understand, and unassailable.

It's not always possible to pin down the exact value of a proposed change. Maybe the information you need to generate an estimate isn't available, or your client doesn't think the effort is necessary. In those cases, look for a qualitative expression of value, such as improved staff morale or some other measure that you can point to if someone asks, "What are we getting from this investment again?"

You may choose to discuss the project schedule in this section, or you may prefer to create a separate section. In either case, consider three steps concerning the schedule. First, communicate about schedule by starting with the general and moving to the specific. Illustrate the overall schedule on a single page so that the entire program is understandable at a glance. This summary of timing would include the major tasks and their dependencies, key milestones, and the planned start and end dates for all activities.

Second, offer a more detailed view of the schedule, especially for complex projects, in an appendix. In this view, you'll expand the summary plan, illustrate the specific tasks, and show who is responsible for each. Depending on the level of detail you choose to show, you may also define the outcome for each task. The objective for this section is to offer a client project manager enough information to evaluate the suitability of the plan.

Finally, be ready for changes to the plan. Once the client reviews your proposal, modifications are likely. Be prepared to discuss how the program would change if you altered the timing or the resources assigned to the team. You may not have all of the answers, but you can think through, in advance, the potential impact of such changes on achieving objectives.

Most sales proposals have some loose ends. You may not be clear on who will be your client contact during the assignment or who will be on the team, so you make assumptions to complete your plan. Whatever (hopefully few) assumptions you make, you can list them in this section. Some writers create a separate section for assumptions, which is also workable. The placement is less important than capturing and communicating your assumptions clearly to the client.

Qualifications

In the qualifications section of your proposal, your readers anticipate learning everything they can about why you believe you have the right stuff for the job. In every other part of the proposal, you are talking about the client. This is the time to talk about yourself, so don't be bashful. But don't waste your readers' time, either.

In too many sales proposals, the qualifications section is an untargeted dump of the selling company's past history. Some sellers seem to think that whatever statement of qualifications they wrote in the past is just fine for the next opportunity—with some minor updating. That notion ignores the power of the qualifications section. If you want to take advantage of this part of your proposal, make sure it has three attributes. First, write it fresh for each opportunity. Naturally, you use previous background material as a starting point, but that's how you should treat it—as a beginning step.

At the core of your qualifications section, write about the most relevant examples of your past work. For instance, if you are proposing to assist an engineering firm redefine its approach to project management, look back at your previous engineering clients and find those that are the best match. How does that work relate to the current opportunity? Maybe the objectives were not exactly the same, but you can find other common points. Highlight the results that you and the client achieved, making sure to give due credit for the client's role in that achievement.

Second, name the specific companies you worked with. If one of them was the Bank of America, for example, say so; it's not convincing enough to say your client was a "global leader in the financial services industry." Finally, offer up names and contact information for the past clients you intend to include in your qualifications. Your buyer may never call those people, but the fact that they are willing to vouch for you may be enough.

It's up to you to decide how much additional information you include in this section about the background of your company, range of services, and any other specifics the client has asked for. But if your qualifications section gets too long, consider creating two sections instead of one. Offer a short, highly targeted statement of your qualifications in the body of the proposal and put the rest in a separate appendix.

You shouldn't make the mistake of taking the qualifications section of your proposal for granted. This is your chance to answer buyers' questions about why they should choose you. Make every word count.

The Proposal Summary

The final section, and by most accounts the most important one, is the overview that summarizes your proposal. After you peek at the price, what part of a proposal would you read first? Most people start reading the so-called executive summary. The dictionary tells us that an *executive summary* is an "overview of the main points of a business plan or proposal." The kind of a summary you see most often is a rehash of what is in the proposal, with an extra dose of seller-centric qualifications.

Given that some decision makers read only the executive summary, use this part of your proposal to knock their socks off. Don't fall back on specious claims. Instead, express the essence of your vision of the client's potential future and a fact-based case for making the change you are proposing. You'll immediately broaden your thinking about your summary if you dump the title "Executive Summary" altogether. Call it anything else—the "Case for Change," the "Path Ahead," the "Imperative for Project X," or the "Future of [fill in the blank]." Your summary doesn't have to be, nor should it be, simply a condensed version of your proposal.

Sanity Check: Rethink the Executive Summary

It's standard to lead off a proposal with an executive summary, that is, a condensed version of the remaining content. But most executive summaries don't influence readers' opinion much, nor do they contribute to closing the sale. Put aside your notions about what you think *should* be in an opening section. Lead with the case for change, not your credentials. Summarize what the clients' future is going to look like if they go with you, not the tools you'll use to get the job done. And talk about the expected value, not your industry expertise.

You want to give buyers the abbreviated version of the story about their future, a path to get there, and why you're the one to take them there. The opening section of your proposal should bring your vision, strategy, and value into sharp focus for readers—in as few words as possible. Show your understanding of the problem with the most important facts. Define the desired future state and how your approach will bring the client to that state. You will go into all this in more detail in other parts of the proposal, so find alternative ways to express the essence here.

Be sure to emphasize value and steer clear of jargon. Some writers want to place long-winded descriptions of their companies in this opening section. Please don't. If you can't resist the urge to say how great you are, allow yourself no more than two sentences at the end of the summary. If your summary connects with your readers, they'll search for more information about you in the qualifications section of your proposal.

More Than a Selling Tool

For sellers, a proposal is a sales document and, eventually, a contract. It's also one of the primary vehicles for conveying your message and recounting the story you have developed about the client's situation. But for buyers, it is more. To them, it is a guide for changing how they run their businesses. If you think about your proposals as a way to offer a valuable solution and facilitate change instead of just a tool to sell you and your company, you'll tap into what clients want, and you'll win more often.

There are two types of sales proposals: those that help you and those that don't. Before you deliver your next proposal, ask yourself, "Which kind is this one?"

PART 3

Commit

CHAPTER 10

The Art of the Sales Presentation

Information is not knowledge.

—Albert Einstein[1]

The last thing most people need in their lives is more information. The paradox of the instantaneous availability of facts, figures, and theories is that the more there is, the higher the walls people erect to absorbing it. The sheer volume of marketing and sales information in the marketplace, for instance, causes most buyers (in self-defense) to block out as much of that noise as possible. So, when you come along with a sales presentation, you have to jump a high hurdle to get buyers to hear your message.

Since people are inclined to filter out most sales information, the goal of a sales presentation should not be just to impart yet more information. Your objectives are to facilitate understanding, to help buyers see their issue or problem in a way that spurs action, to offer alternative solutions, and to make the case for your credentials to do the work. You can't achieve these objectives with presentation techniques alone, whether that's voice control, practiced gestures, or stunning slides.

Instead, your audience will hear you only after you've proven that you have listened and understood what *they've* said. Before most sales presentations, you've probably met with your client sponsor, conducted interviews, researched the company's background, and combed through the relevant documents your client has given you. When it's time for your presentation, your audience members will be evaluating how well you use all that knowledge you gained. If they see you've done a good job, you'll have a receptive audience. If not, expect resistance. As you shape your talk, here are six tips for a compelling sales presentation.

⟶ Tip 1: Never Fly by the Seat of Your Pants

Kevin, an information systems consultant, walked into Brian's office for some last-minute preparation for their sales meeting with a group of prospective buyers. With an hour left before the meeting, Brian handed Kevin a single slide containing three blank, overlapping circles. Staring at the empty Venn diagram in alarm, Kevin asked Brian what it had to do with the meeting.

BRIAN: Venn diagrams help in every selling situation.

KEVIN: They do? How?

BRIAN: This one, for instance, clearly demonstrates the importance of a manufacturing strategy to the financial health of the company.

KEVIN: It's blank, Brian! How can it possibly demonstrate anything?

BRIAN: Because the professor will be there to explain it. We'll fill in the blanks as the meeting evolves.

KEVIN: Oh, and I suppose you're the professor?

BRIAN: Exactly.

Winging it, as Brian intended to do, is the surest way to tank any sales presentation. When you try to get by on your cleverness and charm, you telegraph three important messages to the client:

1. I know what you need, regardless of what I know (or don't) about you.
2. There's no point in exerting effort until I think you might hire me.
3. I am not taking this meeting as seriously as you are.

Some argue that preparation and rehearsal are unnecessary and inhibit on-the-fly creativity in key meetings. Usually, that opinion reflects either profound arrogance or laziness. If you take the stage unprepared, expect a bumpy ride. You may be insightful, but you're more likely to come off as a disorganized mess. For team presentations, a lack of preparation is an invitation to disaster. Sellers who think they are quick enough on their feet to get by on their wits usually end up on their backsides—and losing the sale.

For every sales presentation, know precisely what you want to communicate and how you will introduce, reinforce, and summarize your ideas. Whether it's for a one-on-one meeting or a team presentation, rehearse, at least a couple of times, from start to finish. Pay particular attention to transitions from one topic to the next and to those "white spaces" between speakers. Watch for redundant content, and smooth out all shifts. Be sure each presenter knows exactly where to begin and what to emphasize at critical points.

Have a plan for audience interaction. Whether *you* pose specific questions or stop to take questions from your audience, think about how you'll engage people. With some audiences, you won't need to encourage participation. But in case you have a quiet group, have some method to get people talking, or expect to have a long, boring meeting.

When you have done your homework for a sales meeting or proposal presentation, it shows. Your effort signals that you care about the buyer and the issues, that you want to learn, and that you are committed to the client's interests. By demonstrating that level of commitment, you'll have a leg up on those who want to fill in blank Venn diagrams—and on most everyone else, too.

⟶ Tip 2: Get to *Their* Point

By some accounts, more than 40 million presentations[2] are given every day. Many start off something like this:

"Hi, I'm Mary Dylan from Consolidated Services, and I just wanted to start off by saying say how happy we are to be here and to assist you with this critical effort. In case you don't know about us, Consolidated has five offices in strategic centers around the country. We've been in business since 1985, and our people undergo hundreds of hours of training in seven areas of specialization . . ."

Mary's presentation would likely go into even more depth about her company before moving on to the real reason she was there—the client's issue. Thousands of sales presentations start just like Mary's, and it's out of habit. Sellers are accustomed to and trained to use this type of introduction. Even if the opening is short (which it often isn't), many of your attendees aren't really tuned in. Remember, they do not want to hear about you, even though they may say they do. They really want to hear about themselves. They'll listen to your opening, but they may not really hear it.

Here's another way you might introduce yourself:

"Hi, I'm Mary Dylan from Consolidated Services, and I thank you for your time today. We'll cover three topics this afternoon, beginning with what we know about your issues. We'll discuss that topic and refine our understanding. Then we'll review options for how you might address this issue, with an emphasis on how we can work together. Finally, we'll wrap up with a short review of Consolidated Services and why we think we're well-suited to assist you with this initiative."

With a shift of emphasis, this opening lets your listeners know that their concerns will be up first and that they won't have to endure your spiel until you've satisfied them that you know what they are up against. Once you've done that, don't be surprised if your audience members *want* to hear more about your company.

Here's a rule of thumb for your presentations: Focus on buyers' issues *at least* 75 percent of the time, including right from the start. With conscious effort on your part, a presentation that is mostly about them can still answer all their questions about you, without the usual dull recitation. If your audience doesn't already know the basics about you, that is, your name and company, then supply that information and get on with it. Better yet, have someone else introduce you very briefly.

Should You Give Them Handouts in Advance?

The debate continues about whether to distribute copies of a presentation before the meeting. Some speakers find that handouts help an audience follow along and reinforce the points in the presentation; others feel that handouts distract listeners from paying attention to the presenter. You may have a preference, but let your clients decide. Express your perspective and then abide by their wishes.

Tip 3: Build Consensus Brick by Brick

Though it's a good start, getting to the client's issue right away is not enough to facilitate understanding of your message. Researchers have tested how buyers absorb information in sales presentations and concluded that audience members are more likely to reflect on the case you're making and draw initial conclusions if "messages are chunked—that is, when it is clear where one message ends and another begins."[3] In other words, your audience needs to know where one message or idea stops and the next one starts. Don't make your presentation one long argument and, at the end, ask your listeners to conclude that you got everything right and they should hire you. Instead, ask them to draw conclusions about a series of smaller points to build their final opinions about your offer.

For sales presentations to a group, aim to develop five intermediate "bricks" that call for your listeners to reach conclusions about what they are hearing. These five points roughly follow the flow of your sales proposal. The first four focus on the buyer and the final one on you, the seller.

Brick # 1: The Issue Is Real and Calls for Action

This is where you lay out the issue and reach agreement with your listeners about its nature and existence. You'll want to bring some of your own insights into the discussion to establish your credibility as an expert and to set the stage for why your proposed solution is the right answer.

If, for instance, your client faces rising costs for patient services due to inefficiencies in the emergency room, show how that impacts cost per patient and inventory-handling costs. You may have access to the performance measures of other hospitals to use for comparative purposes, or you can discuss how the industry usually manages this issue. Then get beyond the numbers to the story about how these issues affect the hospital's patients, staff, and investors.

As you lay out your case, look for agreement from the audience along the way. Just because you see the matter in a certain way, don't assume everyone agrees with you. Until your listeners acknowledge that you have this part right, don't think for a minute that they will follow the rest of your presentation.

Brick #2: The Implications

Let's assume that you observe approving nods around the room confirming that the problem exists as you see it. Move on to the rest of the story: the implications of the problem. In a presentation, though, steer away from the blame game about why there's an issue, which can lead straight into a quagmire. Turn attention to how the client's future will unfold if the issue remains unresolved. Some sellers think this means painting a picture of the client's pain and showing themselves riding to the rescue. Forget this self-serving mindset, which can cause you to shade the truth. Besides, it's a transparent sales technique that most buyers will ignore.

Instead, review how the unresolved issue will impact the client's people, operations, finances, and mission. Your view of the future should make the case for change that you have been building throughout the sales process. You're summarizing your earlier client conversations when you ask, "Why this project, and why now?" Be sure to stop for audience discussion. Your goal is to build consensus for action, and you'll inhibit that progression if you leave people behind. Give them the chance to voice their questions and help them draw the conclusion you believe is in their interests.

Where's the Emotion?

As you are presenting the story you developed about the problem and its implications, don't forget the importance of engaging your listeners' emotions, which play a part in decision making, just as reason and logic do. In the book, *Think Again*, the authors point out: "Emotion and cognition appear to affect our behavior through different systems and processes and in very different ways. Emotions are more elemental. They provide the drives that motivate us."[4]

Brick #3: The Alternatives

Before deciding to buy fresh grapes at their local grocery store, most people sample one or two grapes. It wouldn't matter if the produce manager soldered the grape bags closed, *someone* would get into a bag and taste the grapes. One enlightened grocer gave up attempting to stop this practice. She put a sign by the grape bin that said "Try me!" The grocer was letting everyone know that their behavior was just fine.

Services sellers can learn something from that produce manager: Acknowledge that your buyers have choices, and make it easy to discuss those choices. Instead of just presenting what you offer, talk openly about the alternatives. Clients don't expect you to sell a solution other than your own. But you will make your own case stronger if you look into the alternatives, including some you don't offer.

As you review alternatives, start with the option of doing nothing. That is, the client could just maintain the status quo. If you reached agreement with your listeners on the implications of the problem, this discussion should be short. However, it's fairly common to have some clients who believe doing nothing is the right way to go. So get this alternative out there and learn where everyone stands.

Once you've reviewed the do-nothing option, it's time to talk about your ideas for a solution. Presumably, there is someone in the room, preferably one or more client executives, who know exactly what you are going to say, so there will be no surprises. But unless you've agreed otherwise, plan on reviewing several alternative approaches your clients can choose from. Most buyers want options for how they'll manage issues. The monolithic, take-it-or-leave-it approach will turn many buyers off.

Go over the plan you and your client counterparts believe will work most effectively. But don't stop there. Point out at least one other way to resolve the problem, perhaps with a different approach. As you point out the various avenues to resolution, you demonstrate your commitment to the client's interests. Emphasize the pros and cons of alternatives in a persuasive yet objective manner. Encourage examination of each alternative in an effort to build support for the choice that makes most sense for the client. Remember, you want to help buyers make the best possible decision.

As the final alternative, you should mention that your clients could choose another service provider. You won't be able to (and shouldn't) comment in detail about how others can help. Still, you can make reference to the fact that there are others they might want to consider. This is like the "Try me!" sign on the grape bin. It's pretty likely your client is talking to others anyway, so why not acknowledge it?

By guiding your audience through the choices, you give people an opportunity to listen, evaluate, and decide on this aspect of the decision by itself. In this part of a meeting, you'll want to listen to everyone's opinions about the alternatives and come to agreement that you've identified a workable resolution.

Brick #4: Your Recommended Solution

Once you've taken the audience through the alternatives, circle back to your recommended solution. Go into more detail, including the trade-offs, as you see them, that accompany this solution. Emphasize the specific value buyers can expect and what it will take to achieve it. Review the approach you plan to use and how you'll work with the client. Test for agreement among your listeners about your plan.

If you are right about what you are recommending, your presentation logic should flow to an inevitable conclusion. Help buyers understand, one step at a time, the situation, the case for change, the alternatives, and the solution. Many sellers race through the first parts of their presentation to get to the solution. They take for granted that buyers know everything in between. They may know there's a problem, but your job is to bring it to life, at that moment, so they understand exactly what they need to do and why.

Video Yourself

Top communicators never stop improving their skills. They use video feedback to critique their impact on others. Tools are readily available to record your practice presentations. Though videos may not be painless to watch, you'll gain instructive feedback on your voice, mannerisms, presence, content, and delivery style. After a few sessions, you will find specific ways to improve your facility in oral communication. Speaking coaches often use video feedback in their programs. Be sure any speaking coach you hire offers that capability.

Brick #5: Why You?

Now you get to talk about you and your company. But save the details on your company's background until the end of your presentation. Concentrate on the connection between the client's issue and your expertise. Even though your experience may be much broader, talk about your ability to address this specific issue. You won't sway most buyers with your methodology, global presence, or your commitment to the industry if there's not an unequivocal tie between their issue and your qualifications.

Once you get that point across, you can make a few comments about the full depth of experience you bring to the assignment. Presumably, your proposal will cover this topic at greater length. So, in a presentation, limit yourself to what you consider to be the three most important facts about you, your team, and your company.

By chunking your messages, you help buyers absorb information in ways that are most understandable. As you prepare your presentation, outline the logic of all your conclusions. Talk your listeners through that logic in steps, thoroughly and methodically, with a series of facts, stories, and supporting information.

Tip 4: Prepare to Answer Your Toughest Critics

Anyone can handle the easy questions about qualifications and the content of a proposal. To improve your responses to the softballs and to finesse the hard ones, be sure to practice for the toughest questions buyers can throw at you. Your audience will include supporters and detractors, though the identity of each may not be apparent when you start the meeting. And at least one of those detractors (that would be the vocal one) will ask *exactly* the question you were hoping you wouldn't have to answer. Prepare for this eventuality by listing the 10 questions you don't want to answer, and then decide how to handle each one.

Here are three to start with that you should include on your list.

Where'd You Get That Number?

It takes only one, maybe two, misstated facts to undercut any presentation. Like cracks in a dam wall, all it takes is a little more pressure to sweep you right out of the room. Unfortunately, citing your source for every fact may not be enough. You have to show where you got the number *and* why it's relevant to the point you're making. Take this exchange, for example:

CLIENT: Where'd you get that overtime figure for the transportation group?

SELLER: The number came from your company's general ledger.

CLIENT: Okay, but overtime is seasonal. It rises every year at the time you're showing. It's predictable and hardly attributable to the cause you've suggested.

SELLER: You are right about seasonality. To be certain of our interpretation, we conducted an analysis and found that overtime expenses rose to far higher levels in this period than the historic norms. We reviewed the trend with the company controller and the transportation director and got assurance of its validity. If you believe it needs to be adjusted, we can certainly talk about it now, or we can discuss the data after we're finished with this meeting.

You will have sourced and checked the facts for your proposal, of course, but make sure you double-check them before a presentation to avoid embarrassing yourself in front of buyers. And always verify the relevance and meaning of data with someone in the know within the buyer's organization.

Arguing with clients about your conclusions is one thing, and it may even be healthy in some situations. But you *don't* want an argument over the facts, because they are the foundation of your proposed solution. Once the facts are in dispute, you'll have a hard time bringing serious deliberation back to that solution. Try to poke holes in your facts before you start your presentation. Be sure every fact stands up to scrutiny and adds to your case. Otherwise, drop it. There is no reason to jeopardize the entire sale over one disputed point.

Can You Give Us Three Reasons Why You Are Better than Your Competitors?

This may seem like an easy question. If you choose to answer it as stated, you will show your bias and, in some cases, ignorance. For one thing, unless you worked very recently for a competitor, you don't know what the competitor is offering, nor are you really an expert on the competitor's strength and weaknesses. Sure, you've seen some competitive intelligence that indicates your company is better than the rest. But that's not the truth, just facts. And you don't know how your audience feels about your competitors. Maybe the questioner has a preference for a competitor or is alumni of that company. No matter what, you cannot win by answering this question.

Instead, try to reorient the question to one that you can answer. Start by stating your lack of qualifications to make that assessment and then ask if you can describe the three reasons why you are the best to hire. It might go something like this:

CLIENT: Give us three reasons why your company is superior to your competitors.

SELLER: I'd love to do that, but I'm afraid I don't know enough to make a good assessment. I know that my top competitors are reputable and have good people, but I can't say how well thcy would serve you. I do know what my company can do and would be happy to go through those qualifications, if you'd like.

You will not score points by bashing your competitors, so resist the urge. Not only does restraint demonstrate your professionalism, but it also avoids indirect criticism of the buyer's decision to evaluate—and maybe hire—a competitor. Respecting the buyer's judgment, whether you agree with it or not, could be important to the relationship down the road.

Why *Shouldn't* We Hire You?

This question is obviously fishing for an admission of your weaknesses to do the job. Don't take it personally, and don't feel compelled to hang out your dirty laundry. Frame your response with an honest discussion of the trade-offs in your sales proposal. But start off with a confident assertion of your belief that there isn't a reason the client shouldn't hire you. Then ask a question or two of your own to see if particular concerns are driving this line of questioning or if it's just part of the routine.

What does the questioner think might go wrong? If that person's worry is, say, the potential loss of customers as a result of the initiative, talk about how your strategy addresses that issue. Be specific about how you considered each area of concern and developed a plan to account for it. Review your assumptions and seek agreement that the steps you propose will take care of the concern.

Hopefully, you created your proposal with others in the client organization. Don't hesitate to ask one of them to speak in support of your position. Your client contacts are often your best advocates, so use them as a resource when you get into a tight spot.

Again, don't shy away from challenging the question's implication that there are reasons not to hire you. Of course, if there are public matters that could be troublesome, like a pending merger or financial problems, try to get those issues out on the table. The clients probably know about such matters and have an opinion. You can add your perspective, and that could change your listeners' minds on the potential impact of those developments.

Most sellers can make a strong case when the questions aren't controversial, such as those about your understanding of the situation, the proposed value of your offer, and your qualifications. You will make *all* your responses sharper by working through the 10 questions you'd never want to answer. Formulate and practice answers that are honest, spin-free, and defensible. If someone in the audience asks you about a past failure, admit it. The more you dodge tough questions, the tougher they'll get. You may never hear any of the 10 questions you prepare for, but the exercise will make your presentation more confident and persuasive.

Hints for Conference Calls and Web Presentations

Many sellers offer webcasts (or webinars) and teleconferences to establish their credentials, interview clients, and discuss their proposals. Unless you have the technology for live, all-way video, these meetings are especially challenging because you can't assess how you are coming across. Making matters worse, participants are probably multitasking, so they're listening to you with one ear.

The lack of audience feedback calls for more rehearsal than you might think. You don't want to dwell on concepts after the audience already understands. At the same time, you need to explain complex slides more carefully than you might with an audience in front of you. Don't be afraid to use silence. Stop speaking briefly after key ideas to let them sink in. But don't go overboard. Rehearsal will help you figure out how much explanation and silence are enough.

To counter the feeling of speaking into a void, create a mental image of a few listeners and speak directly to them. Allow plenty of time during (and after) your presentation for questions and clarification.

Tip 5: Collaborate on Every Presentation

Every sales presentation has a downside. You'll never be in a room without naysayers, and you may not know all the people who appear at your presentations. You'll have technical glitches; people will come and go; and you'll face tough questioning. You have a job to do: Get your perspectives across, seek agreement, and position yourself to win. You cannot accomplish those goals without help, preferably from the client.

Collaboration with clients on your proposed solution should be an integral part of the sales process, and that includes presenting your solution to others. It's not always feasible, but you should try to involve buyers in the preparation and delivery of every presentation. Solicit their input with the development of the content, and ask for opinions. Get feedback from as many sources as possible. Your objective is to limit the surprises you could face—or that you might create—during your presentation. Find out who will attend your presentation and identify controversial points that need your consideration. If you can't avoid walking into the lion's den, it's better to know ahead of time.

It's not at all unusual for changes to happen on the eve of a presentation, so keep all communication channels open with the buyers. Sometimes, their agenda for the meeting shifts as they hear other presenters, or they may change the attendee list. Maybe your competitor bombed and the client wants you to know what to emphasize and what to steer clear of. In any case, you need that collaboration to stay current on any issue that may affect your presentation.

Some clients won't be interested (or won't have the time) to make substantive contributions to your presentation. Ask anyway. You'll show your commitment to finding just the right answer for the client, and you'll continue building relationships.

Ask for the Business

As you wrap up your presentation, be explicit and ask for the business. Some sellers make reference to their desire to "work with you on this important initiative," but never ask for the sale. They can't say yes if you never ask the question.

⤙ Tip 6: Never Go Second

If your buyers will be listening to more than one sales presentation, try to choose *when* you speak. The order of presentations does make a difference in audience responses. Researchers who studied this concluded that, when buyers listen to sales presentations from multiple sellers, presenting last, especially if it's close to the time of the buyers' decision, confers a powerful advantage. Your ideas gain influence from the "recency effect," meaning that the information people hear last makes the biggest impression. The study also found that sellers who presented between the first and last sellers were the *least* likely to have any advantage over the others. Whenever possible, avoid being the presenter in the unmemorable middle.[5]

In some competitive situations, you can identify a clear market leader and a "me-too" seller, that is, one with a similar offer but less market share. If that's the case, listener reactions to the order of presentations may change. The market leader still benefits from going last, but enjoys a comparable boost from taking the first slot. When market leaders present first, they tap into the principle of *primacy,* which affords more credence to the information people hear first from sellers they *already* perceive to be the best. A lesser-known competitor doesn't achieve a similar benefit from speaking first.

Clearly, if you are sure you represent the market leader in a sale, you should try to present last or, if that's not available, first. Whether or not you are a market leader, you don't want to present in the middle of the pack.

Presentations Are Sales Conversations

Everyone sells at some point in life. Maybe it's selling yourself in a job interview, or attempting to get your spouse to vacation where you want to go. But professional sellers are selling and presenting all the time. Every interaction with a buyer is a sales conversation, whether it's a one-on-one meeting, a phone call, or a major presentation.

You may be a recognized authority in your field and an expert on the services your company delivers, but none of that will matter if you can't master the sales conversations you have every day. Dedicate yourself to improving your ability to communicate with buyers—in every setting. Remember, the people who make this skill look the easiest often work at it the hardest.

CHAPTER 11

Seal the Deal: Negotiating to Close the Sale

You've probably seen or read this scene: Two people sit in a cramped office, hammering out a deal. With a sly grin, the seller slides a folded slip of paper across the desk with the "best" offer. The buyer counters by writing down a new figure and passing the slip back to the seller. After several tense rounds, the two reach an agreement and the deal is closed.

Most services sellers wouldn't dream of trying this tacky technique, but they do resort to other, equally inane closing gambits. The list seems endless and includes the assumptive close, the valued-customer close, and all of the deadline-driven closing techniques. What's wrong with these tactics for the services sale is that a transparent attempt to manipulate a buyer into an agreement endangers what you need most as the sales process wraps up: *trust.* It would be naive to think that buyers don't recognize these techniques for what they are and whose interests they serve—the seller's.

TYPICAL SALES CLOSING TACTICS

The use of manipulative closing techniques is more likely to alienate buyers than encourage them to trust you. Here are some examples of closing tactics that generally backfire with services sales:

Assumptive close: The seller behaves as if the client has already decided to buy by asking such questions as, "Should we fly in and begin work on Thursday, or the following Tuesday?"

(continued)

Valued-customer close: The seller proclaims the buyer's importance to the company and offers a special valued-client concession. The offer may sound like this: "As a highly valued client, and given our long-standing relationship, we'll give you our most favorable rate, which we don't offer to others."

Deadline-driven close: The seller offers an incentive (usually a lower fee) if the buyer agrees to the deal within a certain time frame. The seller may suggest, "We both know this offer makes good business sense, but we can make it even better financially. If you can agree to the sale by the end of the week, I can reduce the contract fee by 10 percent."

That's not to say you can do without the ability to seal the deal. You can't. After all, if you cannot close sales, you won't be in business for long. Think about this part of the sales process as both an end and a beginning. You're working to wrap up the current sale, but you are also (hopefully) embarking on a new phase in the client relationship. You have to balance your need to strike a fair bargain with the desire to keep the client relationship on an even keel. To do that, instead of pushing for a close, think collaboration and shared commitment with your client. Your goal should be a mutually beneficial exchange of value with the buyer. Reach that point, and your buyer will close the sale for you.

Five Principles of an Effective Commitment Strategy

When you and a buyer sign on the dotted line, you are both taking a chance. The buyer's signature represents the ultimate endorsement of your promises; yours signals trust in the buyer's commitment to help make everything work as planned. To navigate the commitment stage of the sale, five principles guide your way.

1. Seek Commitment One Step at a Time

The way you manage the early part of the sales process will largely define how the end unfolds. Typically, commitment discussions with buyers center on fees, expenses, intellectual property ownership, and other contractual terms. And those conversations can be a challenge, no matter how resilient the client relationship. Your goal must be to leave as few unanswered questions as possible for these final discussions.

As you work through the selling process, collaborate with your client to make shared commitments about how you will deliver your services and the role the client will play in that delivery. As early as possible, resolve all questions about the client's role, the decision-making process, and your access to executives. Some negotiation specialists will advise you to agree on the easy parts of the negotiation first. It makes more sense to take care of the easiest issues before you even approach final bargaining.

Speak up about how you prefer to do business. Your sales process should be a learning experience for both buyer and seller. If your company has nonnegotiable items, get them out early, before you head to the negotiation table. Also, review how your buyers like to work with outsiders, the experiences they've had, and how they usually manage the service delivery process. To eliminate surprises that can crop up during final negotiations, explore all facets of the business relationship you're proposing. Fewer surprises will clear the way for more productive discussions of the issues that remain.

2. Articulate a Shared Definition of Value

In one way or another, value is at the heart of every negotiation. If you are buying a car, house, or a vacation package, for instance, how much you value those purchases colors your views on price, financing terms, and extras. For rational negotiations to take place in the services sale, you must anchor your offer in tangible, measurable, and achievable value.

And that should be a shared definition of value with the buyer *before* you begin discussing contract terms. That way, both parties have a basis for evaluating the potential exchange of value. Without clarity about the proposed value of your offer, negotiations tend to drag on and on. You get bogged down defining the value of your proposal—to the exclusion of terms and conditions. A mutual understanding of value serves as an essential arbiter should problems arise in the course of the assignment. If there's a misunderstanding about what you will deliver, that original definition of value points the way to resolution. If the definition is vague, it's likely to add to the problem, not help solve it.

Some sellers complain that it's too difficult (or impossible) to quantify value, so they settle for extolling benefits, like better cash processing or faster candidate recruiting, as a stand-in for value. Once you rely on vague benefits instead of measurable value, your offer looks like a commodity, and you risk getting stuck competing on price. Do the extra analysis to create a realistic estimate of what the buyer stands to gain, and your negotiations will be swifter, saner, and less stressful for everyone.

3. Don't Settle for a Short-Term Win

When they are in negotiation mode, some sellers—and buyers, too—get caught up in a win/loss mindset: For every point in the negotiation, there is a winner and a loser, the reasoning goes. This mindset results in a counter-productive tug-of-war between buyer and seller, who should be looking for common ground instead of fighting each other every step of the way.

Smart sellers don't battle over minor issues, because they know that the fastest way to grow a services business is to sell additional, high-value services to existing clients. So they anticipate a presumed value for the ongoing relationship—and the potential for additional sales—and collaborate with buyers to find an equitable balance. Granted, not all buyers are willing to negotiate this way, but you should be clear in your own mind about how much you value the relationship instead of digging in your heels over mundane contract matters.

One services seller, for example, brought a large sale to the brink of collapse over a disagreement about how the seller would bill out-of-pocket expenses—which made up less than 10 percent of the contract value. The seller's stubbornness had several unintended consequences. First, it delayed approval of the agreement and caused the client to go back over every other clause of the proposed contract. And it led the client to wonder how this seller would behave when something really important was on the line. It's possible to become fixated on the wrong points in the heat of contract discussions. Periodically, pause to analyze all aspects of value, including that of the relationship, and decide if your negotiating posture is helping or hurting you.

4. Negotiate as an Equal

You always want to keep your eyes on the prize, but don't cave in just to get the contract signed. Some sellers are too willing to let a buyer chip away at their end of the deal, hoping the sale will still be worthwhile in the end. This often happens when the buyer's status or leverage in the relationship intimidates you. Regardless of the title, position, or perceived bargaining power of your buyer, you'll strike a better long-term deal if you put aside any preconceived notions about an imbalance of power in the negotiating relationship.

You are not negotiating about people or relative positions, but about *value.* No matter who is at the negotiating table, what matters is the exchange of value. Often, sellers make needless concessions because they mistakenly conclude that giving up on one final point will close the sale, and the accompanying reduction of value for them won't matter in the long run. Without that concession, they reason, the buyer would open negotiations with a competitor and they would leave empty-handed.

That negotiating posture is often rooted in a lack of confidence about the offer's value, not pressure to close the sale. Few sellers, at least not the good ones, willingly concede value without finding some way to rebalance the arrangement between the two parties. Negotiate from the power of the value you bring to the exchange. Your client *wants* to find a way to work with you, so do not underestimate the power of that objective, even when it seems as if the client is about to walk away.

Sanity Check: Don't Assume You Know What They Want

After working with clients during the sales process, you may think you know what they want from negotiations. Some sellers build their negotiation strategies around those assumptions only to find they were mistaken. If you assume you know what your client wants, you're likely to end up negotiating with yourself instead of with the client. Maybe you believe price is a primary concern, so you price the contract lower than you intended to avoid confrontation. You cannot be sure what your client really values until you begin talking about the details. So reserve judgment and put your assumptions aside.

---

5. Be Ready to Walk Away

You will guard against giving away too much only if you are certain of the conditions under which you will walk away. Admittedly, this choice always looks better in theory than in practice. But unless you are prepared to walk, you are not negotiating; you are putting the decisions in someone else's hands and hoping to come out in one piece. Tremendous forces work against walking away, as you might prefer a suboptimal deal to no deal. Still, keep an open mind about this choice and know when to consider it.

If you conduct a thorough sales process, though, you shouldn't need to walk away at this stage. You would have seen the writing on the wall long before the final negotiation. But that's not always possible. You could face a situation, for example, where the client hands over the final negotiations to a procurement executive who wants to drive an unreasonable bargain. You might not see that coming.

You cannot make a decision about throwing in the towel without the clearest possible picture of the value you anticipate from the arrangement. Naturally, financial benefits, such as cash flow and profit, top the list. But, as pointed out earlier, you may have reasons other than monetary ones to choose to work with a client. As you think about negotiating a commitment with the client, you might want to revisit the "Seller Sources of Value" in Chapter 5. Now that you know more about the buyer, the problem, and the situation, you are in a better position to know what you do and don't value in the contact.

Before you negotiate final terms, be sure you understand, in priority order, what you value most (and least) in the contract. Figure out how you might rearrange your priorities if the client asks for changes that impact value for you. Maybe you were banking on the boost of a joint marketing campaign with the client, but that clearly isn't going to happen. What would you prefer instead?

Try on a few scenarios that model changes in what you'd like to receive from the contract. How would those changes impact your view of the contract's desirability? Your goal isn't to decide on a rigid position, but to think about how you could adapt your potential gains to the client's interests. Your prioritized value list will help you manage your own expectations. As the discussion progresses, you'll be able to assess what's happening to value for you and decide how to react. Let's say you want the ability to market the intellectual property you develop during an engagement, but your buyer doesn't seem inclined to agree to that option. Can you suggest an adjustment to another part of the contract to address the impact of that development?

Theresa, a business development specialist for a software firm, was negotiating a contract with Marianne, a long-term client. As part of the deal, Marianne asked for a multiyear, low-cost license for the software firm's proprietary project management methodology. Theresa proposed an exchange of value: The clients would get the favorable license terms if they agreed to jointly fund the effort to develop the next version of the software, which Theresa's firm would retain the rights to sell later. Marianne agreed, and everyone felt they'd found the right deal.

Sometimes, though, you get an uneasy feeling that the number of concessions a buyer wants you to make is getting beyond your comfort zone. At that point, the cost of finding another client may start to look more attractive than the contract at hand. Then it's time to step back and consider your options. You may never walk away from a deal in your career. But knowing what would cause you to take that action serves you well in negotiations. Just be sure you mean it when you say it.

Watch for the Green Light

As you close in on general agreement about a sale, you have to know how to recognize when buyers are ready to talk about the details of the contract. You may not have to do much to move ahead with these negotiations, as clients will sometimes suggest it before you do. If you're not certain the time is right, look for buying signals and then decide how to proceed. Most clients indicate their readiness to move forward by what they ask you. Take it as a promising sign when you begin to hear detailed questions in one of these areas:

- *Timing.* If we need to start on June 1, can you do that? Can your team be available for a preliminary meeting next week?

- *Approach.* Will you be able to use our frontline managers in the training program? Can I have my team review the milestones now and give you feedback?

- *Consultative.* We're considering a new hire to fill the role of our departing project manager. Does that person seem right to you? We're planning a customer communication about the changes we're planning. Would you be willing to have a look?

- *References.* Can you set up specific times for me to call two of your references?

- *Future services.* We also need to consider a program like this for another division. Can you help us think that through?

These and similar buyer questions express a positive level of comfort with you and your offer. When you hear them, don't be reticent; ask about discussing the details of the sale. Tell the buyer how interested you are in the work and that you look forward to wrapping up the remaining points. At this juncture, you should test the client's level of commitment to find out whether you really are in a favored position. Take this exchange, for example:

CLIENT: We'd like to start on July 9. We plan to check your references this week. If those calls work out, is that start date a possibility?

SELLER: Yes, and I will arrange for our people to clear their calendars of other work commitments and be ready for that start date.

If you encounter resistance to that action—lining up specific people— you'll have a better idea how the client views the sale at that point. When you sense no hesitation, you should suggest moving the detailed discussions ahead. But test the buyer's commitment before suggesting that you jump into price negotiations. Selling is about timing. Find the right time to suggest the next step without being pushy—or waiting too long and missing the boat.

Tackle the Tough Stuff First

In any negotiation, some issues will be thornier, requiring more time and effort to resolve. Resist the temptation (and the advice some experts give) to knock off the simple issues first. Get straight to work on the toughest ones. Once both parties decide to get down to the details of a contract, you will have momentum, on both sides, to move forward. Take advantage of that momentum to make the hard stuff your first priority.

Working Out Terms and Conditions

When you talk with clients about contract terms and conditions, keep a few things in mind. Most clients aren't unreasonable, but sellers have taught some of them to be when it comes to negotiating. For decades, sellers have cut deals, offered discounts, and used every sales trick in the book to get a client to say yes. By now, clients expect some sort of deal. Experience with salespeople has conditioned them to behave that way. They readily believe that your first offer is bogus and represents only a starting point.

Why shouldn't clients ask for a better price? They've gotten more for less that way in the past. Besides, if they do ask and you say no, what's the downside for them? Of course, some buyers want to work with you but truly have budget constraints. You'll recognize those people because they will be working diligently to come up with an agreement that works for everyone. And then you will encounter others who are unaware of (or don't believe in) the value of what you have to offer. You'll need further discussions about what you're proposing to do—or why they can't do it just as well without you—before they come around. If you find yourself frustrated by tough negotiators, remember how they got that way.

Not that you need this reminder, but the most common points of contention in contract negotiations are about financial arrangements: price, support costs, expenses, and the like. Most often, you hear three kinds of buyer objections to these arrangements:

- *Price.* "The cost is too high."
- *Execution.* "We're not sure you can do this."
- *Self-interest.* "We want it all."

Price: "The Cost Is Too High"

Buyers will often ask you to reduce your price. Don't be surprised if some ask you to lower the fee in the early part of a contract, with the promise of a fee increase in later phases. Or you may hear requests to put a cap on fees, or to bundle fees and expenses together. Another tactic is to appeal to your ego by saying, "You are the best. We would love to work with you, but we have only this amount to pay you." All these positions have a common element: The buyer, understandably, wants to get more for less money. Take this scenario, for instance:

CLIENT: If you can reduce the price by 15 percent, we're good to go.

SELLER: I understand your desire to keep costs down. I'm happy to lower the price by 10 percent. If that works for you, we can start as soon as you'd like.

CLIENT: Okay, tell you what. Let's split the difference and reduce the fee by 12.5 percent.

SELLER: Great. We look forward to getting started.

This response, splitting the difference, may seem like a reasonable way to resolve a tricky situation, and it pops up in all kinds of negotiations. But for selling services, it is one of the *worst* strategies you can use. For starters, it establishes a precedent for negotiating on the basis of price, not value. You can easily give away too much by agreeing to an arbitrary reduction in your fee.

You can also expect the buyer to base all your subsequent negotiations on price. What's worse, you create an environment of mistrust, as buyers will wonder what they left on the table when you went along with the compromise. They'll ask themselves how straight you were being about your initial price and how much lower you would have gone. Such suspicions can cause buyers to ask for deeper discounts in the future. And, to be sure that they are getting the best possible price from you, you can expect to see even more competitors for the next contract. Clients will want assurances that they are getting a fair price, and they'll "keep you honest" by asking others to bid.

In response to questions about reducing your price, ask your own questions. Why does the client believe the fee needs adjustment? Is it a budget issue or a misconception about value? Once you understand the reasons behind the request and get the client to acknowledge them, too, then you can decide how to proceed.

When facing a request to lower your fee that is not just arbitrary posturing, you have at least three options to consider. First, you can examine the scope of the work and look for areas to trim, thereby balancing the reduction in value for both buyer and seller. Instead of rolling out your program in all of the client's offices this year, maybe you could postpone some until the next fiscal year, when there's a new budget. Second, you can change your approach to shift some of the costs from you to the client. Perhaps you can modify the staffing model to let the client handle more of the tasks than originally planned. Or you may have options to change the schedule in a way that allows for a reduction in cost.

Third, you can look for new ways to make the project more attractive to either the buyer or the seller. If you've done a good job in your earlier work, you should know the sources of value for your proposal. Be creative and attempt to find (or create) others you didn't think of before. You must always be thinking about more sources of value for the client, so don't stop asking questions about how to boost that value.

Sometimes, small things make all the difference. In one negotiation that stalled over price, the seller was probing for additional potential for value, and the buyer jumped on an idea: It could tip the scales in favor of the deal if the seller's CEO agreed to make a visit to the client's office. The CEO in question was well known in the client's industry, and a visit would create substantial buzz and offer the client's executives a chance to meet and discuss business strategy with an industry leader. That idea for a single visit took the price reduction request off the table, and the seller won the work.

Execution: "We're Not Sure You Can Do This"

Though buyers are usually most concerned about price, some may be uncertain about whether you can pull off the planned results. As a hedge against problems, they may ask for a fee based on specified performance benchmarks, such as program milestones. That way, they slow payment for your services until they have sufficient evidence of your capabilities. Other clients want to delay payments until the work is under way to make a contract more cash flow friendly for them. The best sellers are not surprised by this request, as they discuss it with buyers early in the sales process.

Before you respond to this request, once again, you need to question the reason behind it. Do the buyers have legitimate concerns about your ability to deliver, or are they just aiming to make the timing of payments more palatable to their accountants? If it's the latter, you should be able to dispose of the request with an appeal to reason. Uncertainty about your ability to deliver is a more serious concern, which may be due to a lack of knowledge about your risk-mitigation strategy. Offer to review the program plan, discuss how you will measure progress against the plan, discuss the team and its qualifications, and offer to let the client call more references.

Self-Interest: "We Want It All"

There will be times when you run into negotiators who want it all: a lower fee, faster delivery, performance- or milestone-based pay, expense caps, and generous payment terms. They'll threaten you with an eager competitor they claim will meet every request. If you end up facing this type of a negotiator and it's a surprise, you may have mishandled earlier parts of your sales process. As you progress though the process, add to your understanding of the client's environment so you can envision the likely scenario for its end.

Most sellers don't have a problem with tough negotiators as long as they are raising honest concerns. But some negotiators aren't. They throw everything, including the kitchen sink, at you to keep you off balance.

By attempting to extract acquiescence with an exhaustive list of demands, their objective is to make the two parties seem so far apart that only major concessions from you can close the gap. You can try questioning the source of each demand and discussing options for resolution. Unfortunately, that's probably not going to work. You can't win if you're playing checkers and the buyer is playing winner-takes-all poker.

The biggest drawback to this negotiating scenario is the damage it can do to client relationships. If you respond in kind to an intractable negotiator, you're not going to look very good to the client when it's over. Remember, the name of this game is looking out for number one, and this sort of negotiator will do anything to make that a reality.

You have three options to manage this type of negotiation. The first is to stick it out, take your lumps, and try to get an agreement. In some cases, the initial bluster from hard-nosed negotiators subsides once you establish rapport with them on the issues. Second, you can use a third-party negotiator. Some sellers use professionals to negotiate terms and conditions, and such proxy agents usually recommend that the primary salespeople stay away. That allows you to preserve the collaborative bond with the client even when contract talks become acrimonious.

Last, you're back to this: You can walk away. If you can't find mutually agreeable grounds to work together, you might as well call it quits and move on.

Getting Commitment

Transforming a prospective client into a paying one requires you to be a highly capable seller *and* negotiator. But there's no magic formula for becoming either one. Every situation you face has its own nuances. What doesn't change is your need to grasp those nuances so you can seal the deal. And that means asking questions—lots of questions—to understand your buyer's motivations. That knowledge will help you create the right value for you and for your buyer, at the right price. Just remember, you are not only winning the sale, but building the relationship, and your business, for the future.

CHAPTER 12

What to Do When You Win . . . and When You Don't

"We liked your proposal, but . . ." When a buyer starts a conversation that way, you'd probably rather endure a multihour airport wait than listen to the rest. Once you hear, "We're going with another company," your first impulse might be to try and swing the apparent loss to the win column. Through questions and clarifications, some sellers have been known to persuade buyers to reconsider a decision. If nothing else, try to keep the door open for the future by asking whether it's okay to stay in touch. It's rare for a client to say no to *that* request, which represents a small victory.

Even if the decision to use another seller is final, there's a wealth of market intelligence buried in that decision, and it's too valuable to leave unearthed. Yet, in an extensive study of sales practices, only 26 percent of responding sales professionals agreed with the statement, "Win or lose, we get accurate feedback on all proposals from our customers."[1] Why do so few services sellers get this feedback? For some, the reason may be the pressure they feel to move on to the next opportunity. Others may be uncomfortable asking a client to explain a decision, especially if it was a rejection. To improve your odds of winning in the future, you have to face up to the reasons behind clients' buying decisions.

You Can't Win 'Em All

Your first reaction to a loss may be to assume you know why the contract went to someone else. But maybe you lost because the client hired the boss's nephew, not because your proposal was inferior. Or maybe the clients decided to do the work themselves. You can't be certain that you know what really happened. So, when the client calls with bad news, ask if you can schedule a follow-up meeting, in person or on the phone, to explore ways you can improve your approach. Most clients recognize—and appreciate—the resources you put into your sales process and are willing to cooperate. Give yourself some time to absorb the news, and then draft the interview questions that will help you learn what worked and what didn't.

You can start with some form of "The Client Perception Survey" shown here. Notice that it emphasizes familiar components of the sales process, including the value you proposed, your team, approach, fees, and qualifications. Your goal should be to uncover one or two areas of strength and some areas for improvement. For each factor on the survey, ask the client to rank both its importance to the buying decision and how your team performed on that factor. You *could* create and print up a survey form and ask clients to fill it out; but you're likely to get better feedback if you talk through these questions instead.

WHY YOU WON OR LOST: THE CLIENT PERCEPTION SURVEY

Whether you win or lose, get client feedback in the following areas. Customize questions for the topics you deem most relevant to the sale. Using whatever scale works for you, ask clients to rank each factor in two ways: (1) its importance to the decision and (2) how well you and your team did on that factor.

PERFORMANCE FACTORS

Expertise

- Our expertise in your industry
- Our expertise on the issue you're facing
- Trust in the team's capability
- The team's ability to diagnose the problem and devise a solution
- The team's analytical capabilities and creativity
- Our methods and tools to get the job done

Solution

- The proposed approach to the assignment
- The relevance of the proposed solution
- The quality of our sales proposal

Terms and Conditions

- The fee for services
- Other terms and conditions, such as expense policies and payment terms

Company Qualifications

- Our company's track record
- Our company's support of your needs
- Comments from references
- Quality of our company's thought leadership
- Availability of other services you might need

Sales Process

- Design of the sales process
- Team's ability to work effectively with you
- Clarity of the team's communications

And one final question: What would you suggest we do differently in the future?

Pay particular attention to factors the client says were important or very important in the decision but on which your team didn't meet expectations. Those will be the critical areas for improvement. The final question asks how you can do better in the future. The answer will often reveal the truth behind the other responses. Clients may rate your team as exceeding expectations in general, yet still think the team members don't know enough about how to operate in their organization. Comments like these are the most useful; they help you and your people grow from the experience. Also, such feedback provides hints regarding how you should expect the client to evaluate you in the future.

Finding the Gap

Maybe you lost because the winning company had an obvious built-in advantage, such as favored status with the buyers. Or the loss might be due to failed chemistry between you and one or more decision makers—a common occurrence, by the way. If those two reasons don't explain the loss, you can usually boil it down to a gap the buyers perceived between their needs and your abilities. You need to understand the cause of that gap and close it next time.

During the sales process, the buyer's perception of your ability to meet the need at hand defines the value of your offering. That perception reflects two basics: your understanding of the situation and your proposed approach to creating value. Even slightly misinterpreting an aspect of the client's environment can leave you with a flawed—and losing—approach. Of course, most sellers confirm their understanding of a problem before devising an approach. But it's easy to wind up a victim of your own assumptions.

It's also possible that you performed flawlessly but the client preferred your competitor's ideas. For that reason, make sure your client debriefing includes open-ended questions like, "Can you summarize three reasons why you didn't go with our proposal?" In most cases, clients will have an answer ready for this, but don't be dismayed if it conveys less-than-blazing insights. As a skilled interviewer, you should be able to read between the lines and frame your next questions to elicit more useful responses. For example, if the buyer says that your proposed team was not well enough qualified, ask which team members met the standards and which did not. If you hear that your pricing wasn't competitive, ask about pricing alternatives the buyer might consider in the future.

This line of questioning should allow you to check most of your assumptions. Be sure to cover the client's view of your approach, if that doesn't come up on its own. It's possible to comprehend objectives yet miss the mark in your approach. Ask for the client's view of your people, work plan, schedule, and tools. Perhaps a team member wasn't a good fit; maybe the way you planned to organize the effort wasn't ideal for the client. It's equally possible that your assumptions about the client's desired level of involvement led to an unrealistic schedule. By engaging the client in a discussion about what you might have missed, you may find new ways to offer your services down the road.

What about Price?

For some clients, choosing a service provider is solely about price. In some instances, the lowest bidder wins, even if a better alternative is available. On the other hand, some clients select sellers based on price because they can't discern any difference between the competitors. That's a misconception you can correct.

When buyers say, "Your fee was too high for our budget," it may not really be about budget constraints. Instead, they may not find the value-to-fee ratio compelling enough to explore options for boosting the budget. Price is an important consideration in every selection process. But a higher-priced competitor can win if the client's perception of value justifies the fee. Again that perception depends on both your demonstrated understanding of the proposed initiative and your ideas and capabilities to get the work done.

Will you get straight answers in a loss review meeting? Maybe. It can be painful for buyers and sellers alike to sit through such discussions. Some clients will sidestep your questions to get the meeting over with as soon as possible, while others will bare their souls. In either case, you're only looking for a few areas to work on, so it's worth the investment of time, even if some people are reluctant to talk.

When you hear, "We picked another company," you will feel deflated. After all, most sellers pursue sales they believe are winnable. If you expend the time and effort to submit a proposal, the last thing you want is for a competitor to walk away with the business. But you can turn today's loss into tomorrow's win by eliminating guesswork and getting the story straight from the buyer, not your imagination. What you imagine is probably much worse than the truth.

No one likes to lose. Try to keep your reactions in perspective and determine what you can do about it. You may find that you gain more valuable insights from a loss than from a win, although it's clearly more flattering to hear about why you won.

The First Thing to Do When You Win

When you win a contract you worked hard to land, you may feel elated and challenged at the same time. You are elated because your hard work to forge client relationships and demonstrate the value of your offering paid off. But a sense of foreboding may not be far behind. Now you have to convert the expectations you set during the sales process into reality.

The transition between the completion of a sale and the beginning of an assignment marks the greatest challenge to the success of the initiative—and to the future of the client relationship. At this juncture, the actions you take will define the project as one with clarity and momentum, or as one that stumbles off the starting block. And, although an assignment that starts slowly may gather steam as it progresses, it will almost always finish behind schedule and over budget.

Once you get the final nod from the client, your thoughts should be about what you can do to avoid a slow start. Before you charge down that path, though, first take time to learn precisely why you won. Just as with a loss, chances are you think you already know why. But until you hear it from the client, it's all speculation. If you plan to sell more work to these buyers, take advantage of the opportunity to find out how and why they chose to hire you. Those answers can give you a leg up in future opportunities and can help you refine your approach to selling to other clients.

You can use the client perception survey to understand what was important in the client's buying process and how your team performed. Seek out your client sponsor(s) to help you collect this feedback. Many buyers have strong opinions about how the selling process went and are eager to share their views, assuming you get to them soon after you win the work.

Responses to the survey should give you a clear view of where your process succeeded and where it fell short. For a point of reference, pretend you are the client and take the survey yourself. You might find that it adds an interesting perspective. You will be tempted to think you know all the answers about why you won, but don't rely only on your own opinion. One seller was convinced that the key to a win was the quality of the extensive proposal the sales team spent countless hours creating. It was a complete surprise to find out that three of the key decision makers didn't think the proposal was that great. Those opinions almost cost the team the job. And they didn't know it until after the fact.

Define the Client Experience

When you change gears from selling to delivering services, both you and the buyer are bound to be wondering, "Now, how are we going to get this job done?" No matter how well you laid the groundwork during the sale, expect a barrage of questions and concerns. While the dust is still swirling, get off to a flying start by defining, with the client, the precise way you will work together to achieve the desired results.

How will you structure the effort to create momentum and a great experience for the client? Your clients will look to you for leadership on how to proceed, so don't wait for their questions. Get to work immediately planning how you'll organize to deliver everything you promised. Be sure to look back at the client value profile you created earlier. You can bet your clients will remember any commitments you made during the sales process, so be sure your plan accommodates those commitments.

You may have a particular way you want to deliver your services, and most clients will go along with that. Even with a standard approach, though, you need to calibrate your service delivery process and pace the work so that your client moves along with you. If your work moves faster—or slower—than your client's ability to make decisions, for example, that will impede your overall progress. Promising rapid results without regard for the client's pace of work can lead to real problems. One seller, who was coordinating a series of client site visits to several facilities, was stymied by the client's delay in helping arrange the visits. These pivotal meetings, which were supposed to be a one-week task, took more than a month to complete, resulting in a three-week delay in the early going.

You may believe your proposed schedule is realistic, but temper that opinion with your observations about how the sales process worked. Did the client make decisions and commitments quickly and on time? Did events move as you expected? During the sales process, clients give you clues about their future behavior. Use those clues so your service delivery plan is compatible with the reality of the client's situation.

It isn't unusual for clients to convincingly promise to pull out all the stops for you. They may say they will fast-track all decisions and make resources available exactly when you need them. And they may come through. But wait for a demonstration of that follow-through before you bank on it. Your clients still have a business to run and that will, and should, take precedence over anything you need to do.

Work closely with the client to verify the contributions you'll each make to the effort. Stress continuous consensus on the essential elements of success: communication, managing people, decision making, and expected outcomes. The guide that follows, "Defining the Client Experience," outlines discussion points for launching your assignment with success. By covering these points with your client, you leave nothing to chance.

DEFINING THE CLIENT EXPERIENCE

Before you and the client jump headlong into the work you need to do, set aside time to go through these questions. How will you . . .

- Determine who will assume which roles and responsibilities on the client and the seller teams?
- Obtain client agreement on the proposed plan to complete the work?
- Introduce the service team to the client?
- Integrate the client and seller team members with one another?
- Define expected outcomes and make sure everyone knows when you achieve them?
- Set up milestones to accelerate early progress and keep momentum?
- Manage internal communication and reporting?
- Handle external communication to suppliers and customers?
- Establish frequency and timing of progress reporting?
- Make key decisions?
- Add or remove resources from the assignment?
- Conduct the work on-site (and at any other location), including work space and telephone access?
- Bill the client?
- Hand off the finished product to the client?

In the history of services delivery, you can find no end of stories about embarrassing miscues (for instance, team members not knowing about the kickoff meeting, executive sponsors who were away on vacation at critical moments, and service providers showing up to work with no place to sit). Early missteps can derail an engagement and strain client relationships. But you can head off most problems with in-depth discussions that clarify purpose, tasks, communication, and outcomes. Maybe the client managers need to temporarily relieve some people of their regular duties to help with the initiative. Or perhaps they can find ways to rearrange tasks more efficiently.

These early efforts also help you with another challenge. As an outsider, you are committed to creating client value, so you have responsibility; but in the hierarchy of the client's organization, you have little (or no) authority. Your success rests largely with others and on your ability to influence the actions of those who may have no accountability to you. This requires leadership skills, and the best sellers rise to the occasion. You should be able to motivate people with the story of why they need to address the problem and what things will be like once they take care of it. Use that narrative as a way to keep everyone, especially the client's people, focused on the objective.

Your most powerful tool of influence in the client setting is, of course, your own behavior. Set the example by holding yourself accountable. Work with others to be sure they can be successful, and step in to pick up the slack when problems arise. If you lead by example, most people will follow. If you show a confident dedication to results, so will others.

Sanity Check: Be Overresponsive

Clients may be hypersensitive to problems that surface early in an assignment, even if they seem like minor matters to you. The service delivery process can be messy, with some fits and starts, but most clients are ready for that. They won't, however, tolerate even a hint of chaos in how you are managing the effort. In most cases, that perception results from a lack of communication, not any serious dysfunction. Still, be overresponsive at the beginning. Keep those communication channels wide open and stay visible and accessible. And don't assume that clients are going to remember everything you told them or that they know what to do. After all, they have other priorities pressing on them. More attention at the outset may well save your sanity later.

Set Milestones

You can accelerate your start, mobilize people, and create momentum by setting short- and long-term milestones. You rarely get people to settle down and get busy on an assignment until you set the first deadline. To solidify everyone's sense of purpose and commitment, you want to create a culture of accomplishment. Establish an early, tangible milestone and you'll have a way to foster such a culture.

An early milestone helps people learn to work together and puts to rest nagging questions about details. Everyone gets a look at how the team performs under pressure, which can help managers adjust their plans, if needed. The trick is to make it an early milestone. Consider using a week or so for your first deadline. A short deadline helps iron out the wrinkles, allows the team to establish communication patterns, and builds anticipation.

As beneficial as a first milestone can be, the last one is even more critical. Before you launch any initiative, you and the client must define *done*: How will everyone involved know that you have achieved a successful outcome? Of course, this definition can shift over time. But establishing an explicit ending milestone takes the mystery out of the question "Are we done yet?" Few things inspire confidence more than setting a clear goal for the finish. The clearer that goal, the easier it will be to rally your team around its achievements.

Know What You Want to Get

Throughout the sales process, you focus on the clients' needs. But your work isn't just about them—it's about you, too. So don't lose track of your own goals for any job. What would be a perfect outcome from this assignment for your business? Satisfied clients and winning additional work aren't acceptable answers. Those responses are givens.

Reflect again on your professional development goals and business objectives. Remind yourself what new skills you'd like to develop or new people you'd like to meet. Maybe you see a great case study, article, or speech emerging from your work. You should review the sources of value summary you prepared during negotiations. Envision reaching those objectives, and you'll be even more excited about your opportunity.

Once clients say yes, your immediate job is to prove they made the right decision—because they *are* wondering. It's likely that you've built up a store of goodwill with your client, so be sure not to squander that precious asset with an early mistake. If you design a positive client experience, establish a compatible pace of work with your client, and find productive ways to influence the actions of others, you'll be well on your way to the real win: a closer relationship with your clients and a shot at their next sale and beyond.

CHAPTER 13

Making the Second Sale and Beyond

Once you have work for a client running smoothly, you have another decision to make: whether and how you want to work with this client again. With an existing client, you may uncover new demand for your services, potentially with less competition and lower cost of sales. Until you've tried it, selling to existing clients may sound easy. It's not. For sellers who choose to attempt it, though, the rewards can be substantial.

Some sellers say they make every effort to sell new work to their current and past clients—with inconsistent results. They point to their account management plans and insist they stay on clients' radar, yet that only brings leads they would have heard about no matter what they did. And those leads are as competitive as any others they pursue. So why invest any more in account management?

You can't argue with such poor results and, unfortunately, most account management programs won't yield anything more worthwhile. Why? One reason is that most programs are transaction focused. The seller does make a systematic effort to stay in touch with the client, but only with the next sale in mind. Most clients see right through that. You can invite your clients to events, include them in mailings, or call them once a month. But if, in their minds, it all adds up to just another sales pitch, don't count on extraordinary results—no matter how great a client relationship you think you have.

What's wrong with most account management programs is that they are true to their name: They manage accounts, not relationships. The programs are seller-centric and include objectives such as gaining the largest share of the client's spending on services and pushing a specific set of solutions.

You'll hear some sellers describe their account management strategy as "penetrating the account," "gaining wallet share," or, worst of all, "eating what you kill." If you think clients can't sense the mercenary attitude behind those strategies, you are dead wrong. Such approaches have an ironic consequence: They cut you off from the very flow of information and executive access that could support a relationship management strategy.

Once you've landed a sale, trying to take more and more is counterproductive. Yes, you want to build your business, and working with your current clients is the best source of new business. Your clients understand both of these realities. But with existing clients, you must give to receive. Many sellers understand this in theory, but they insist on giving the client what they want to give, not necessarily what the client needs. You can drown people in fascinating white papers, case studies, and invitations to fancy conferences. But if those items aren't exactly what the clients need at that moment, where's the value for them? It's a waste if all that effort just ends up in the round file.

What Is Client Relationship Management?

To make the second, third, and fourth sales, you need to think about managing relationships with people, not accounts. As pointed out before, your goal must be the long-term success of your client's business, not the next sale. On your first assignment or two for a client, you will, hopefully, lay a foundation of trust and competence and demonstrate your commitment. Clients will then be more receptive to your ideas and may ask you to bid on new contracts without a competitive proposal process.

Account Management versus Client Relationship Management	
Account Management	**Relationship Management**
Transaction selling	Long-term relationship
Competition for each sale	Preferred supplier
Vendor status	Business adviser
Service focused	Solution oriented

The goal of your client relationship plan is to find new ways to help your clients manage their businesses. That means using your knowledge of the client's priorities and the resources of your company to offer ideas, strategies, and tactics that address the client's greatest challenges, even if those offers don't lead to a specific sale for you. If your contributions are meaningful, the work will eventually flow your way.

Naturally, clients expect you to advance ideas for new initiatives that you can support with your services. For instance, a tax adviser, in the course of preparing a client's return, might spot an opportunity to minimize future taxes and might propose to conduct a study to explore the possibility. Similarly, an accountant might detect a weakness in a client's management reporting system and suggest improvements. Once you've established a trusted relationship with your client, you'll be able to surface genuinely useful ideas. And the client will need your expertise to act on some of those ideas.

Again, the real test of your commitment to the client's well-being, though, is whether you raise issues and ideas for services that your company can't provide. The best client relationship managers don't hesitate to suggest another resource if it serves the client's interests. In fact, they assist the client in locating the right service provider.

Client Relationship Management Defined

Client relationship management is a systematic approach for building a mutually beneficial, advisory relationship with a selected group of clients.

Cultivating Strategic Relationships

Does developing a long-term client relationship sound like a lot of work? Well, it is. To do it well, you must invest time and effort not only to cultivate relationships, but also to search for sources of value for clients beyond any immediate initiative or sale. Most sellers can't afford to lavish that much attention on every client, at least not if they want to stay in business. You have to determine which relationships to designate as your strategic ones. Then decide how to advance those relationships.

Think about how the airlines stratify their customers and you'll get the basic idea. Airlines single out their most frequent patrons (who are also the most profitable) for special treatment. They are entitled to seat upgrades, express check-in, and other perks to lessen the hassle of air travel. And the airlines segment that group of frequent travelers even further, which determines the level of service. Services sellers must make similar choices about client relationships. It is well worth the investment to dedicate long-term resources to some relationships; for others, it just doesn't make sense.

Choosing strategic clients, that is, those you will invest the most effort in, means considering the success of their businesses and yours, too. To help you choose, answer these six questions about each of your clients:

1. *Does this client offer profitable, long-term opportunities?* You should not make strategic investments in clients if you answer no or maybe to this question.

2. *Does the client's business fit with your long-term market strategy?* If the client is in the aerospace business, and you're not planning to emphasize that industry in the future, think twice before allocating resources to a strategic relationship.

3. *Will the organization's executives be a good source of referrals?* You'll want to be sure you can build your network of contacts. Your strategic relationship accounts are an effective way to do that.

4. *Is the client likely to need help in the areas of your specialization(s)?* Even if no immediate opportunities are available, you should be able to anticipate whether the client will have future demand for the services you offer.

5. *Do you like working with this client?* It isn't important to share exactly the same culture, but it is important that you can work effectively together.

6. *Does the client support your efforts and want to work with you as a strategic client?* If you answer no or maybe, this client isn't the right choice for a strategic relationship. The client has to be receptive to the idea, too.

For each client, compare and contrast your answers to these questions. If you have numerous clients to evaluate, consider weighting each question and creating a rough scoring method. That will narrow down your list by eliminating some candidates. Once you do that, review the remaining clients on the list to decide which ones offer the best chance to match their needs with your capabilities.

> ## Sanity Check: A Big Contract Doesn't Equal a Strategic Client
>
> Some sellers use the sales revenue generated by a client as the primary decision criterion for investments in strategic relationships. Just because a client awarded you a high-value sale doesn't mean that the client should be part of a strategic relationship program. Be sure the client meets your predetermined investment criteria before making that decision. That way, you won't spin your wheels investing in relationships that won't work for you or the client.

Keys to Successful Client Relationships

For Randall, the client relationship began during a short project for the smallest division of a health care organization. Randall's team, plus two client managers, worked on the four-week assignment, gathering data, conducting analyses, and searching for sensible conclusions. The resulting report recommended three actions the client could take immediately to resolve the current dilemmas. Randall and his team brought insights, value, and realistic solutions. They easily surpassed the client's expectations for the quality and thoroughness of their work. But the client didn't ask Randall and his team to implement the recommendations they worked so hard to create.

Even so, Randall stayed in touch with this client. He regularly researched the latest topics in health care management and sent the client summaries of his most relevant findings. He offered a quality assurance review for the implementation the client had not invited him to work on. And he introduced his client to people in the industry who had completed similar projects successfully. Randall was sure that he and this client were a good fit. He had a specific plan for the relationship, and he stuck with it.

Then, more than a year later, the client asked Randall to submit a proposal for a multiyear organization redesign program, which his team eventually won. From that point forward, and for several years, Randall's team had first right of refusal on almost every initiative for which the client sought outside assistance. Randall's long-term success was no accident, but rather the result of his consistent plan for serving the right client— without an apparent opportunity on the horizon.

As with any business venture, you should not head into a strategic client relationship effort without a plan. It can be elaborate or not. Just make sure your plan expresses what the client will get from you, what you want to achieve, and the investment you need to make. Without those basics as a guide, you risk giving up before you achieve your goals.

Always start with what's in it for the client. Improve your understanding of the macrotrends impacting the client's industry and company. Review that information from your earlier work with the client, and make it your business to keep up to date on the client's world. Just as you did in preparing for the sales opportunity, build your base of knowledge around the client's key stakeholders (customers, employees, suppliers, shareholders, and regulatory agencies). You'll want to keep an eye on the company's financial position, strategy, and management structure. With that data, you'll have a good idea of the potential areas where you might be of service.

Next, inventory your client relationships. If you completed a client value profile (see Chapter 7) during your sales process, you should already have what you need. If not, make a list of the people on the client's management team that you'd like to get to know. For each person, assess how well you know the individual, your take on the status of the relationship, and what you believe each person needs.

Finally, prepare a schedule of activities that you believe will bring that all-important value to your clients. Use a planning horizon of nine months to a year as you think about ways to engage with your clients. That could include attendance—as a speaker or participant—at industry events, periodic briefings or meetings on topics of interest, or offering support for other activities the client has planned. And don't forget to keep the client up to date on changes in your company, too.

✓ Extend Your Reach

To establish your credentials to assist your client with other opportunities, build your network of relationships within the client's organization. Find ways to expand your reach and knowledge of the client by meeting with managers and executives you don't know. Don't limit yourself to the department or division you're working in; think about how you can also meet people in other parts of the company.

Some sellers will tell you that they already do all of these things. They may call it "client face time," "making an appearance to wave the flag," or something similar. But these interactions are centered on the seller, who checks in with the client to see how things are going and maybe to take the client to lunch. The discussion rarely strays from the seller's latest offering or small talk. Once the meeting ends, the client doesn't think about that seller until the phone rings again in the next quarter.

In contrast, consider Dana's story. He had three strategic clients he kept a watchful eye on. He had a relationship plan for each organization, which included his assessment of needs and a plan for how he wanted to grow his relationships. He kept in touch and offered to meet over lunch or some other event, and his clients took him up on those invitations every once in a while. But he also offered his clients a periodic briefing on the latest happenings in their industry, particularly changes in government regulations.

Dana's briefings were informal but concise, and he always followed up with a written summary. He offered specific suggestions for how each of his clients might handle upcoming changes. The resulting dialogues helped Dana learn even more about his clients and their industry. Dana's clients never skipped his briefings, because they knew he wouldn't ask for a meeting unless he had something of value to say. The quality and depth of the information Dana shared with his clients separates his actions from those of most sellers. And Dana often left those briefings with a new sales opportunity.

For Dana, the keys to success were patience and perseverance. He invested his resources wisely over time to transform individual assignments into long-term relationships, which resulted in years of uninterrupted sales. Armed with a plan that stresses value over the sale, you can beat the dreaded feast-or-famine syndrome. You can smooth out the spikes and dips in sales that many services sellers have to endure.

HOW TO END A CLIENT RELATIONSHIP

It goes without saying that you have to execute your assigned work with unparalleled excellence to stay in the game. But relationships often boil down to minor things, too. Make any of the following mistakes, and don't expect the client to invite you back.

(continued)

- Be ill-prepared for an important meeting.
- Go over your client sponsor's head to expedite a decision.
- Come off as just a seller.
- Take sides in interoffice squabbles.
- Waffle over decisions.
- Take the last cup of coffee in the office kitchen and leave the pot empty.

⌒ The Obstacles You'll Face

That's not to imply that a strategic approach to client relationships will ever be a snap. For one thing, it can be awkward to keep in touch on a regular basis, especially if you are not currently working with the client. And you will lose relevance for the client if you drop out of sight for months at a time, making it even harder to reconnect. In an interview in *Management Consulting News*, consultant and author Ford Harding points out reasons why sellers have difficulty staying in touch with clients:

> One rationale for hesitating is the natural question: What reason do I have for calling this person? That's a major concern when people begin this activity. It almost disappears by the time they've been doing it for a year.[1]

You must be creative to uncover insights your clients want to hear about. In addition, you need the discipline to make the client calls or visits and do the inevitable follow-up from those meetings. Understanding that these activities are necessary isn't the problem for most sellers. Making the time is part of the challenge; the rest is about confidence. In another article, Ford Harding says:

> A big part of rainmaking is persistence. Several times a week a name comes up on my tickler system of someone who has not responded to previous calls. And still, after all these years, the little voice inside me says to give up, that it is not worth the effort, that the person doesn't like me and doesn't want to talk with me. It is by learning to override that voice that I have become successful.[2]

It may be accurate to say that selling to a strategic client, or any existing client for that matter, results in a lower cost of sale than selling to a new one. But your current clients are bound to set the performance bar higher for you. It's typical for clients to demand far more knowledge and insight from their preferred service providers than from a seller they don't know. You'll need to integrate that knowledge into your sales proposals and create more value than your competitors. Also, don't be surprised if your clients believe you can work faster than a newcomer. After all, your knowledge of the company's people, processes, and systems should you give you an advantage.

That expectation of higher quality rises as the client relationship deepens, and it extends to whatever you do for the client. You may get a pass on a mistake or two, but you'll wear out your welcome unless you excel in everything you deliver. If you experience hiccups on any assignment, plan to see more competitors showing up for the next opportunity. Never forget that your client relationships are only as strong as your competence to deliver what you promise. If an assignment swerves into the ditch, you'll see how fragile a client relationship can be.

You will find it easier to overcome these obstacles if your company is fully on board with the strategic relationship process. Sales managers often press sellers to "meet their numbers" in the short term, but an investment in a client can pay outsized dividends in the longer term. That means finding ways to reward top sellers (or at least avoid penalizing them) for investing in strategic relationships that help grow the business.

Sanity Check: Relationship Managers Are Not Interchangeable

For strategic clients, it's best to arrange a single point of contact for the client and stick with it. Some sales organizations are too quick to swap out their relationship managers. Often, they do so because they believe there is a better use for an individual—for example, a new sales opportunity. But making a swap can cause confusion and stress for everyone. Worse, it may lead to clients' indifference about the person you're assigning to work with them.

Like a stock portfolio, not all strategic client relationships will work out as planned. Some relationships will exceed expectations, while others will disappoint. But if you balance your client portfolio, and your relationship managers are competent, you should boost sales at a better margin than you'd get with new clients.

Most services businesses can benefit from identifying and cultivating strategic relationships. With the trend toward reduction in the number of providers that clients choose to work with, it's practically a necessity to zero in on the interests of the clients you can do the most for. To make strategic relationships productive, you must learn to spot new demand for services that clients genuinely need instead of waiting for them to come to you.

If you can make the shift in thinking that's required to manage a strategic relationship, you'll be ahead of most sellers. Managing strategic relationships instead of sales should lead to consistent, profitable demand for your services, and with less competition. That's great work when you can get it.

PART 4

Challenges

CHAPTER 14

The Seven by Seven Seller

Max is a rainmaker by anyone's definition. He uncovers and sells enough profitable work to keep a large practice of service providers fully employed, year after year. His sales lead stream is full of qualified opportunities in good times and bad. Max seems to have natural advantages over others. People trust him immediately; he grasps core issues facing buyers almost instantly; and his ability to synthesize everything he's learned and come up with just the right answer keeps him in high demand. Max doesn't overtly sell anything. But clients buy from him.

Some people think Max's success is the result of a "sales gene" that few mere mortals possess. It's true that he is articulate and demonstrates a high degree of empathy with others, but his skills and market presence evolved. He *became* a rainmaker.

— The Service Sellers' Path

One of the enduring myths of selling is that the most successful sellers were born for the job. It's as if they landed on the planet with an innate ability to sell. You've probably seen gifted sellers in action, and you may have bought something from one of them. But the best sellers, like great leaders or orators, aren't born that way. If you turned back the clock on Max's career, for example, you'd see that he started off with a short list of contacts and a rudimentary understanding about what his company offered. He had raw talent, but few sales skills.

Today, service sellers must develop their capabilities at a time when the relationship between buyers and sellers is undergoing radical transformation. Buyers are demanding ever more knowledgeable, solution-savvy sellers and real-time responses. They want salespeople who are subject-matter experts and who know as much about the implications of solution implementation as they do about selling.

For sellers, these developments demand a corresponding transformation of their function in the sales process and in the skills they need. To thrive, today's services sellers must assume the roles of business adviser, idea merchant, strategist, and project leader, among others. And to excel in those roles, they must master the broad set of skills outlined in this book, including client interviewing, problem diagnosis, solution development, and interpersonal communication. Taken together, there are seven roles and seven skills that define the new "Seven by Seven Seller."

The Roles and Skills of the Seven by Seven Seller	
Roles	**Skills**
Business adviser	Client relationship development
Idea merchant	Interpersonal communication
Strategist	Client interviewing
Project leader	Problem diagnosis
Change leader	Sales proposal development
Relationship manager	Project management
Communicator	Personal selling, negotiating, and closing

To be a top seller in the current environment, your mindset must transcend the singular objective of closing the sale. Instead, your goal must always be the improvement and growth of your clients' businesses for the long haul. And that means embracing the seven roles of the new services seller *and* acquiring (and constantly refining) the seven skills you need to star in those roles. The seven skills don't correlate on a one-to-one basis with the seven roles; rather, these seven skills support you in various aspects of the roles you play in the services sale. First, here's a look at the seven roles.

The Business Adviser

Today's businesses are so complex that few (if any) professional service offerings work in isolation. If you provide advertising services, for instance, you work with client managers from sales, marketing, communications, and other parts of the organization. Your eventual success depends in part on your ability to absorb the details of the business and come up with an advertising solution that will meet the client's needs and objectives. To do that, you study the client's business, strategies, and goals before you design a program. You ask yourself how this solution might fit in with the current operation of the business and with its future. In other words, you set aside your role as seller to function as a business adviser.

Instead of making assumptions about a buyer's need, you diagnose the client's need in an impartial way. And, in close collaboration with the buyer, you devise a range of workable solutions, which may include services offered by other sellers. If your services are not the right fit for the client, your job as a business adviser is to make that clear—without feeling as though you're doing the wrong thing for *your* business.

The selfless act of referring some business to another company—or suggesting that the client doesn't need to do the project at all—elevates your stature in the eyes of your client. You no longer appear to be a self-interested outsider, but a service provider searching for the solution that works best for the client. Demonstrating that your interests are congruent with those of your client is imperative to building trust, which is the bridge to winning subsequent sales.

The Idea Merchant

Selling professional services always begins with an idea. Most often, the idea is a way (or ways) to solve clients' problems or improve their businesses. Today's clients are curious about the world outside of their organizations and hungry for ideas that can make their businesses ever more effective. You can be a conduit for those ideas, thus becoming your clients' go-to resource. That is, you are the first person the client thinks to call when your subject comes up. To fill that role, you must be willing to continuously build your subject-matter expertise on top of your service expertise.

If you offer services to improve sales lead management, for instance, you naturally need to know the ins and outs of your solution. But you also have to demonstrate a high level of expertise in the broader business concerns of those who manage sales forces. That includes understanding emerging trends for sales organizations, how others manage similar issues, and how the latest research impacts your clients.

That level of expertise is not easy to maintain; it takes diligence and a genuine passion for the subject. But once clients recognize you as a subject-matter expert, they will call for your ideas—and for your services. Differentiate your company and your offerings with your creative ideas.

The Strategist

A good strategist sees the entire picture. Beginning with shaping the rationale for a client project, you envision how to implement the solution and what value will flow to the client as a result. In collaboration with clients, the strategist addresses the complex organizational issues that often emerge during a sale, including such concerns as how to most effectively integrate the service with other initiatives and who the right person is to lead the program.

For example, if a client wants to reduce the number of the company's suppliers, you must consider the general management concerns, such as the impact on the client's workflow and supplier negotiating strategies. By offering a broader view of the implications of your service, you provide what clients really need and will pay for—workable advice for managing their businesses.

The seller's role as strategist also extends to planning every step of the sales process itself. As with any business venture, a complex services sale is rarely successful without a workable strategy, and it's the sales team's job to put that together. A typical sales lead begins with an idea, whether it comes from you or the buyer, that has an objective but few details. Often, there's a notion of value, but only a rough sense of how to pursue that value or what the implications might be.

In response, you assess the buying environment and the client's issue to make an important strategic decision about whether to invest resources in the potential sale. If you decide to proceed, you design a strategy to win a *profitable* sale. That means identifying what you're selling, to whom, and what resources (including which people) from your company will be involved.

—— The Project Leader

Once you have a viable sales strategy, your skills as a project leader are tested. That's because the complex services sale is more than a sales effort; it's a project in itself. And, like a project, each sale has its own objective, scope, timing, staffing, and budget. Buyers rightly view the sales process as a dress rehearsal for how you and your team will operate if you win the job. As all great project managers do, you operate with a vision, communicate widely, and manage tasks to meet specific objectives.

In your role as a project leader, you must also make the best use of your resources, including proposal writers, industry experts, and company executives. You may find that managing the internal dynamics of your own organization is the most challenging management task you have to tackle. So keep everyone at your office aware of the status of the sale, the challenges your team faces, and your strategy for winning. The role of project leader is a balancing act that accommodates the needs of the client along with those of your business.

The Change Leader

You already know that a successful sales effort brings significant change in how clients do business. Because of that, your ability to guide the client through change is as important to the sale as the quality of your service offer. And you can see why: In the past, too many clients witnessed the erosion of promised value when a seller's implementation approach resulted in delays or, worse, project failures.

Clients learned this lesson well. Now, they're not just asking questions about what will change, they also want to know what you will do to minimize the disruption. Today's sellers must influence not only *what* must change, but also how that change will come about. That's why your service offer must include a well-organized approach to change, including communication programs, education initiatives, job redesign, and approaches for measuring postimplementation performance.

Some sellers claim that an "approach to change" is the signature feature of their services offers, but history tells another story. The business lore is full of initiatives that failed to meet their objectives because the important issue of leading change wasn't handled with appropriate care. Being a change leader means that you work with the client in an open and honest way to assess every aspect of change and offer practical approaches for guiding the client through the change.

The payoff for this behavior is far more valuable than a near-term sale. You earn goodwill and trust, which will lead to winning the second sale—and many more.

The Relationship Manager

None of the seller's roles is more important than the others, but without the ability to excel at building client relationships, you'll struggle to stay in the game. The other roles you play—business adviser, expert, strategist, project manager, and change leader—provide the necessary foundation for relating to clients. Not by chance, those who master these roles are usually also the best relationship managers.

Building relationships during a sale is essential, but those efforts accelerate once you close the sale. After you and the buyer agree on the terms of a sale, aim to create more value for the client and seek productive client interactions. First, revisit the people you met during the sales process to keep them apprised of progress, answer questions, and follow up on any issues. Mostly, you want to be sure the client is heading into the effort with a positive view of the team, but you also want to offer assistance, as needed.

Second, plan for the new relationships you'd like to initiate. Use your knowledge of how you will roll out the service to meet those who will be most affected by the change. Set up meetings to preview the upcoming plan and offer insights on how things will change. The primary goal is to smooth the way for the implementation of your service, but you can also use these meetings to introduce yourself and your company to those who may not know you.

Finally, the best relationship managers expand their networks into other parts of the client's organization. Even people not directly affected by a company initiative can have a keen interest in what's transpiring. That reality gives you a reason to meet others and offer them something they want.

You may wonder whether clients see these networking activities as sales pitches in disguise. That's certainly a possibility, and clients are conditioned to suspect your motives. But top sellers always base their reasons for meetings on the client's interest. If you are a subject-matter expert who also happens to sell, rather than a seller who has some expertise, you will find buyers who are willing to listen.

⎯ The Communicator

There's rarely such a thing as an easy services sale. Some sales just close faster than others. But it remains the primary responsibility of the seller to negotiate the sale with favorable terms. Each of the preceding roles offers ways to establish stronger client relationships and manage the sales process, but those roles only facilitate the sale. To bring a prospective sale from a lead to closure demands expertise in persuasive communication, building trust, and, as important, asking for the sale. To excel in this role is to succeed in all of the others. And to do that, you must master seven specific skills.

── Mastering the New Seller's Skills

Embracing the seven roles of the services seller is the first part of the equation for success. What remains is for you to address the "Seven Skills for Sales Mastery" that you need to excel in those roles. You'll find that the seven skills apply broadly *across* the seller's roles. Don't look for a direct mapping of skills to roles. To be effective in client settings, you must have all of these skills. By developing a plan and taking action to master the seven skills, you set a sound foundation for long-term success and, in the process, become that go-to resource for your clients.

THE SEVEN SKILLS FOR SALES MASTERY

Top sellers cultivate a core set of professional capabilities that allows them to operate effectively in a complex sales environment. They master skills in seven areas:

1. *Client relationship development.* Offer strategic thinking and planning for clients' long-term benefit; establish trusted client relationships based on recognized expertise, innovative ideas, competence, and a mutual exchange of value.

2. *Interpersonal communication.* Lead discussions and influence direction and outcomes; exhibit active listening and questioning skills; communicate effectively at all levels in client organizations.

3. *Client interviewing.* Prepare for and conduct insight-based discussions with client executives and others to gather relevant facts to support the development of a winning services offer.

4. *Problem diagnosis.* Use analytical techniques to uncover the root cause of client problems; envision a range of viable solutions.

5. *Sales proposal development.* Convey a persuasive written view of objectives, approach, economic terms, and expected value.

6. *Project leadership.* Plan and direct the sales activity of the seller and client teams from initiation of the sales process until the sale is completed.

7. *Personal selling, negotiating, and closing.* Offer compelling reasons to spur action, in both one-on-one and group settings; propose and obtain agreement on terms and conditions that serve the client's needs and preserve the seller's profit.

Sellers know they need ongoing professional development to accelerate their careers, yet they often struggle with how to design strategies for themselves. Most sales organizations offer traditional sales training programs that provide the basis for an approach to the services sale. What's often lacking is the recognition that each person enters these programs at a different stage of professional development and that each has a different level of competency in the seven skills.

The ideal starting point for planning your acquisition of selling skills is an honest self-assessment of your strengths and areas for improvement. Examine your last three sales efforts, especially how your performance reflects on each of the service seller's seven roles. Then, answer four questions:

1. Which parts of my performance in each of these roles worked well and which did not?

2. What elements of the sales process made me the most uneasy, and why?

3. What feedback did I receive, directly or otherwise, that offers clues about how others perceived my performance?

4. If I could change one thing about my performance, what would it be?

Begin with what you did well and are comfortable with. These point to skills that you should plan to refine over time, so give those areas a lower priority for short-term development. Next, make a list of what made you uneasy or what you would have done differently if you had another chance.

You may find this list difficult to create. Sometimes we see strengths in ourselves where others see weakness, and vice versa. To get past that problem, rely on the feedback you received, both formally and informally, during your past few sales experiences. Were there specific comments from colleagues or clients that could help you recognize what you're doing well and what needs improvement?

Maybe your presentation style isn't as polished as you'd like. Or perhaps you're not satisfied with your client interviewing skills. Whatever the case, capture these ideas on a short list as your highest priorities for professional development. Use the guide that follows, "Mastering the Skills of the Professional Services Sale," to identify the topics for your skills development. It's not likely that you can tackle all of your goals at once, but put together a plan that spans 18 to 24 months.

Mastering the Skills of the Professional Services Sale	
Services Sales Skill	**Primary Competencies**
Client relationship development	Principles of strategic thinking Client account planning and management Fundamentals of cross-selling
Interpersonal communication	Design and delivery of small and large group presentations Strategies for persuasive communication Effective storytelling
Client interviewing	Principles of planning and conducting fact-gathering sessions Hypotheses design and questionnaire development Effective one-on-one questioning techniques
Problem diagnosis	Fundamentals of problem solving Analytical techniques for problem analysis Methods for conveying findings and conclusions
Sales proposal development	Persuasive writing techniques Managing proposal development teams Principles of effective sales proposals
Project leadership	Project planning and management Communication in a team environment Team leadership
Personal selling, negotiating, and closing	Understanding the service buying process Techniques for estimating expected value Principles of sales negotiation

As you think about how you'll accomplish your aims, consider all of the training tools available to you, whether those are seminars, books, podcasts, webcasts, or others. You'll also want to decide which roles in the sales process you want more direct experience with; you will want to target those areas in your next sales opportunity. You can attend every selling seminar ever offered and not learn as much as you will by working with clients. To make those client experiences valuable learning ones for you, you have to figure out, before you begin, what skills you are after.

Be sure to follow the traditional methods of goal setting to stay on track and motivated. For each role you want to improve on, you'll want to have a specific objective, a list of actions you plan to take, and when you'll complete your actions. Then, don't put the plan aside. Keep it with you. Plan all of your daily, weekly, and monthly activities with your professional development goals in mind. Don't let those goals slide when the next client emergency comes up.

Sanity Check: Sell until You Drop

Some people say that you won't achieve success unless you dedicate every waking moment to your career—nights, weekends, and holidays. Without a doubt, the service seller's life can be demanding and unpredictable. But if you let the job overtake your life, career burnout is sure to follow. You must be dedicated, motivated, and, at times, willing to drop everything at a moment's notice. But don't lose track of what's most important in your life.

What the Rainmaker Does

Achieving a consistent level of sales success takes practice, and that means observing, participating in, and leading sales efforts. Just as you can't learn how to sail a boat by reading a book, you won't pick up the essential skills of selling without experience. But if you don't supplement your experience with the wisdom of others, through books and other sources, colleagues who do will pass you by.

Top sellers continually improve their skills and knowledge. They never stop trying to get better than they were last month or last week. They don't miss a chance to learn more about their area of expertise, sales strategies, or even current events. They attend industry seminars to broaden their knowledge; they listen to audio programs, podcasts, webcasts; and they read—a lot. When some sellers are relaxing between sales, the top performers are still going full tilt to make the next round of client meetings more valuable. Between sales opportunities, you're likely to find them interacting with past clients, working on a new idea, or catching up with industry developments. They may make selling look easy, but most rainmakers work harder, and more productively, than average performers. But they also know when to shut it off to keep some balance in their lives.

You've probably heard the self-limiting expression, "You're only as good as your last sale." It's true that you are always proving yourself in the sales business. But with the right plan and actions, you can be sure to always be *better* than your last sale.

CHAPTER 15

Putting It All Together

O n a nondescript street corner in Portland, Oregon, sits the secondhand store, Fairly Honest Bill's. As you approach the storefront, you get a preview of exactly what you will get inside. The store's exterior signage declares, "If you don't like the price, too bad." If you think you can haggle to get a better deal, forget it. Another sign informs you that "No reasonable or unreasonable offers accepted." Fairly Honest Bill (his legal name) does not equivocate. He claims only that "What you see is what you get."

F. H. Bill gives buyers what they want most from sellers: the truth, stated unambiguously. Most service sellers try to do the same, but many buyers don't see it that way. They are wary, wondering whether they're getting the real deal or a bill of goods. In response, sellers tend to overcompensate by talking about value, value, and more value, in the hopes of winning the buyer's confidence. Sometimes, those claims are spot-on; other times, the seller is "all hat and no cattle," as the saying goes. The unfortunate side effect is that a client's expectations of value can grow beyond the seller's ability to deliver. And if the service falls short of its promise, the client becomes disillusioned and even more leery of future claims from service providers.

That's not to say that sellers are solely to blame. Buyers may hear what they want to hear and thus are responsible for at least some of their own inflated hopes. Whatever the cause, neither the buyer nor the seller wants a poor outcome. But it still happens too often.

Sellers who break this cycle of doubt build stronger, more enduring client relationships and businesses. If you are known for telling the unvarnished truth, maybe delivered a tad more tactfully than Fairly Honest

Bill, *and* you bring superior expertise and competence to clients, you will win more sales, and at a higher profit. One challenge for sales organizations is how to find and grow those top sellers, which is a vital mission for any sales organization.

What Makes a Great Seller?

Finding top salespeople is tough enough, but the task is even more difficult if you're not sure what you're looking for. It's not costly to analyze what makes a top seller great, especially when compared to the resources organizations devote to hiring and training. But very few organizations do it.

Research tells us that most of the sales organizations involved in complex sales are not sure *why* their top sellers excel, and they are not leveraging that success to help others improve. Only 42 percent of sales executives agreed with the statement, "We know why our top performers are successful." Even fewer (26 percent) of their salespeople said *they* understand what top sellers do differently. Among the most successful sales organizations, 45 percent said, "We leverage the best practices of our top performers to improve everyone else." For less successful sales organizations, that figure falls to a dismal 21 percent.[1]

Clearly, there is room for improvement, and the stakes are high. If a sales organization can land just a few more great sellers (and develop the ones they have), they can transform their fortunes. Bringing in talented sellers often raises the level of sales performance across an organization. Not only do rainmakers bring in more business, but their performance inspires others to aim higher. On the flip side, a poor hiring decision has the opposite effect.

Finding just the right person can be a daunting task, because many hiring processes won't uncover the real superstars. Too many sales managers make hiring decisions based on their intuitive "feel" for someone's selling ability, not on a careful evaluation of talents, skills, and behaviors.

It's common to hear veteran sellers proclaim that they can size up *any* candidate in just a few seconds and know if that person has what it takes to make it. Not only is that initial perception often wrong, but it rarely offers any insight into how a person will behave in selling situations. To find your next great seller, look for candidates who possess the personal traits you believe are important and who can thrive in the stressful business of sales.

TRAITS OF A TOP SELLER

How do you spot a rainmaker (or know if you are one)? The ideal seller is:

1. *Curious*. Actively seeks knowledge and divergent views, but knows when to stop asking questions and take action.

2. *Persistent*. Follows a problem or issue to its logical conclusion; is not easily discouraged.

3. *Disciplined*. Has an orderly thought process and develops sound strategies for pursuing sales, but doesn't blindly adhere to rigid methodologies.

4. *Adaptable*. Handles ambiguity and change during a sale or an assignment with ease; doesn't lose track of desired outcomes; demonstrates a high degree of patience, but doesn't tolerate unnecessary delays.

5. *Able to work independently*. Is comfortable working alone, but functions just as well in a team environment; understands the potential power of a team effort in selling.

6. *Self-directed*. Tackles work and develops new skills with minimal guidance; takes the initiative for self-improvement, especially in subject-matter expertise.

7. *Courageous*. Takes appropriate risks, but knows when to ask for an assist; makes decisions confidently, bringing others along in the process; always behaves with integrity.

8. *Smart*. Sees the big picture and all the moving parts and connections, but isn't smug about it; is a quick study in new situations.

9. *Socially aware*. Is cordial and gracious without being a glad-hander; able to articulate positions in a direct, sympathetic manner; perceptive about how change impacts people and their needs; keeps a sense of humor.

10. *Analytical*. Assembles facts from data and correctly intuits meaning.

(continued)

11. *Objective*. Dispassionately considers every option for a problem, but settles on a workable solution; maintains a fair and balanced view, even under pressure.

12. *Creative*. Draws inspiration from all experiences and conceives new ways of looking at situations; is imaginative without getting lost on tangents.

Which of the 12 traits of a top seller make the most sense for your organization? Once you decide that, design an interview process that probes for those traits and calls for the candidate to illustrate them through behavior. Most often, you can learn about these traits by examining three qualities in every applicant: intellect, personal behaviors, and motivation.

INTERVIEWING FOR SALES BEHAVIORS

To figure out whether you have a top seller, ask situational questions that test for evidence of desired traits. Here are some sample questions to get you started.

INTELLECT

- *Articulate*. Can you describe an occasion when your communications skills prevented a problem that seemed unavoidable?

- *Common sense*. Have you ever had one of your commonsense solutions adopted instead of a more complex recommendation?

- *Judgment*. Can you illustrate a situation when you made a judgment call that the data didn't necessarily support?

PERSONAL

- *Collaboration*. Did you ever opt to collaborate with others even though you could have done the job or task (maybe even better or faster) by yourself?

- *Risk taking.* What risks have you taken that didn't work out as you'd hoped?

- *Self-confidence.* Can you think of an occasion when your confidence in yourself and your judgment allowed you to take action?

MOTIVATION

- *Client-focused.* Can you describe a time when you solved a client problem that was beyond the scope of the work the client hired you to do?

- *Goal-oriented.* Are there any goals you have worked toward that others thought you couldn't achieve?

- *Self-motivation.* What personal development activities have you undertaken on your own initiative?

When it comes to intellect, you're not searching for the next Einstein but trying to get at this: Is this person bright, articulate, and intuitive? It's easy to get a general sense of how smart someone is an interview; what counts is the individual's ability to apply that intellect to diverse situations. You can readily find highly intelligent people with no self-awareness and lots of ego, and they will almost always hurt you in selling situations.

To assess an individual's likely behavior in those situations, which is what you really must learn, pose specific problems for solution. Use examples that let you see how a person thinks under pressure and organizes a response. Maybe you disguise a difficult sales situation you faced in the past and ask how the person would address it.

As you consider possible questions to test intellect, ask those that call for the person to use creativity. When presenting the problem, eliminate obvious remedies from consideration. Explain several solutions that the client already tried, and then ask the candidate to come up with a different remedy. Once you get a response, pose follow-ups: "How would you develop this solution?" "What constraints are important to consider?" "What else would you need to know to be sure of your answer?" Some people will ace these scenarios; others will experience meltdown. You can guess which ones you want on your team.

Sanity Check: What Questions Are You Hearing?

You can save yourself time (and grief down the road) if you pay close attention to the questions an applicant asks. As you present a problem scenario, does the person jump right in with an answer or seek clarification first? Top sellers don't assume they have all the facts as soon as they hear a client's explanation. They pick up on the salient points and always verify their understanding. Look for that tendency. If the candidate doesn't ask relevant questions, let that be a red flag to learn more about how the person will behave when solving real problems. Otherwise, you could end up with a dud.

Next, evaluate personal behaviors to appraise the individual's ability to excel in a client environment. To know if you have a potential star, you want to assess the person's patience, empathy, work style, and tactfulness. To evaluate patience, for example, ask about an instance when the person remained patient while others were chafing at the bit.

Listen carefully to how the candidate describes the situation and its outcome. Is it compatible with how you *want* sellers to behave? How did the person fit into the situation—with a leading role or a following one? Did the candidate take the opportunity to make an impact when others didn't? Are there other ways the applicant could have handled the matter? The further you delve into the details, the better sense you'll get about the individual's behavior and its impact on others.

Many interviews end up being about times the applicant was the hero of the story. In fact, interviewees often relate one of their success stories each time they hear a question. It's fine to hear about those occasions, but you also want to know how the person behaves when things don't go as planned. You'll learn more about an individual's true behavior by asking about setbacks than by listening to victory stories. Ask the candidate to describe an important (work-related) loss. All sellers have stories about the one that got away, no matter how much they would like to forget about it.

When you ask about a sales loss, expect some reticence from the candidate, but push ahead. And don't settle for a story in which the person played a bit part. Ask about a time when the individual was essential to the sales process, but still lost.

Then assess the candidate's answers. What were the person's reactions? How did the candidate (and the sales team) interact with the client? What degree of responsibility did the applicant take for the loss? How did the sales team work together during, and after, the news of the loss? Did the applicant treat everyone involved with respect? How did the person make decisions about how to proceed as the sales process moved ahead?

The third, and final, area of evaluation is the prospective seller's motivation. Most salespeople *are* motivated to work hard, but that's not enough to succeed in the services business. You're looking for people who channel their motivation so they grow professionally and reach their potential through the strength of their own convictions. The next time you hear someone talk about being ambitious or wanting to get ahead, look for the proof. What sacrifices has the person made to pursue an ambition or dream?

Some of the traits to explore concerning motivation include persistence, enthusiasm, resourcefulness, and commitment. One way to uncover these is to ask about personal victories. What *non-work-related* accomplishment is the person most proud of? You may have to wait through a long pause before someone responds to this question, but the answers are always revealing.

Follow up to ascertain why this was such an important accomplishment and what the individual did to face the challenges it took to achieve the goal. This line of questioning shows how the person approaches adversity and takes action toward a goal. Your assessment of these traits is essential to figure out whether the applicant has what it takes to develop into a top performer.

Your aim in evaluating past behaviors and experiences is to get beyond the rehearsed answers that applicants prepare. If you can get someone talking about behaviors without a script, you get a glimpse of the real person. From that view, you can use your own judgment to make a well-informed analysis of the candidate's ability to grow into tomorrow's top seller.

Once you've made the decision to hire, the real work begins. Many diverse skills are necessary for sellers to star in all seven roles of the services sale. Sales managers must work closely with each seller to create professional development plans that will allow their people to fill the roles and master the seven essential skills described in Chapter 14.

Developing Sales Superstars

Whether you are a business development manager, vice president of sales, principal, partner, or have any number of other titles, you are *the* enabler of your salespeople's growth. Individual sellers take their cues from your behavior and actions. You may hire exactly the right people, but for them to become top sellers, you need to show them the way. Too many sales organizations throw new people into the deep end of the pool—inside a knotted burlap bag with weights in their shoes—to see how they perform.

Give every seller a head start to success with specific steps. First, begin with your service offer. Every sales organization stresses the need for sellers to understand their services, but take that introduction a step further by emphasizing both the capabilities and the limits of your offer. Once your sellers have mastered the basics of your services, show them what really works and what doesn't. Use specific examples of how other salespeople have adapted their services to accommodate the unique situations that sellers often see. Show them successes *and* catastrophes. It's often easier to see what can work well when you see what went wrong. Remember, they will eventually learn where your services have soft spots. Let them see those areas early and learn from them before they lead a client down the wrong path.

Next, assist your salespeople with building the internal and external relationship networks they need to grow. Encourage active participation in industry or civic groups. Offer opportunities for sellers and their colleagues to interact outside the context of the latest proposal. Just as you build trusting relationships with clients, find ways for your salespeople to develop a network of trusting relationships with colleagues. You'll boost their productivity if they're not meeting the supporting sales cast for the first time when a new sales lead emerges.

Also, design specific, regular programs for salespeople to understand their roles and to master the seven skills of the services sale. Typical sales training usually emphasizes managing the steps in your sales methodology and persuading a client to buy, which are important. But, today's services sellers need much more. To address the gap, offer learning opportunities (and time) for skills like client interviewing, problem diagnosis, and solution development.

"The Roles and Skills of the Seven by Seven Seller" in Chapter 14 can assist your efforts to design a training strategy for your services sellers. Offer customized paths for each person so that all your people reach their potential, at their own pace. Let your sellers take responsibility for their professional development by choosing what skills they need to develop and when.

To help guide career development choices, pair every seller with an experienced mentor who will serve as a sounding board for client or professional development issues. Many organizations use mentoring programs, yet fail to get the full benefit. Too often, these programs serve only as a way to pass along information to people about their job performance and pay raises. When mentoring has authentic backing from an organization, it fosters a culture of collaboration for the sales team, provides a way for newer people to add skills, and challenges the more senior sellers to stay at the top of their game.

A strong culture of accountability must be the basis of any effort to develop and mentor your sales team. It takes time and patience to develop a great salesperson, but you must make tough decisions about which people will thrive in the culture and which will not. Poor sellers hurt you in the market, and they encourage your top performers to question your motives. So put as much effort (or more) into evaluating your salespeople as you do in searching for the next great salesperson. Reward top performers well, and give others support to improve. If you make a hiring mistake, take appropriate action and move on.

No matter how much training or on-the-job experience you offer your salespeople, their greatest source of inspiration is you. They'll watch your every move to make sense of acceptable behavior in dealing with clients and colleagues. You set the tone as a leader, so behave in the way you want others to act. Offer your salespeople access to individualized education, effective mentoring, appropriate on-the-job training, and a positive role model, and your sales performance will soar.

Parting Thoughts for Sellers

There's no doubt that the relentless pace of change in the ways we do business and sell services will remain a fact of life. What won't change, especially for the complex services sale, is the need for consultative sellers who can form resilient client relationships based on competence and mutual respect. By embracing the concept of the Seven by Seven Seller and following the Three Cs of Winning the Professional Services Sale, you can meet any sales challenge you face today or tomorrow and keep your sanity in the process.

Some perspectives on salespeople endure in the sales lore in spite of their irrelevance or wrongheadedness. If you've been around the sales profession much, you've probably heard someone tell a story about a great salesperson who could sell refrigerators to Eskimos. While humorous, that image represents everything you *don't* want to become. The ability to sell *anything* to buyers, whether they need it or not, may seem impressive in a way, but it's also a sure path to ruin in selling services. Instead, live by three simple rules: Build authentic relationships with colleagues and clients; never stop learning; and when you know a client really needs what you have to offer, go for the sale with everything you've got.

Introduction

1. From the movie, *Jaws*, Universal Pictures, 1975. See http://en.wikipedia.org/wiki/Jaws_(film).

Chapter 1

1. Woody Allen quote is from www.tompeters.com/entries.php?rss=1&note=http://www.tompeters.com/blogs/main/010477.php.
2. From the movie, *Jerry Maguire*, TriStar Pictures, 1996.
3. Robert Cialdini interview, "Meet the MasterMinds: Robert Cialdini on *Influence*," *Management Consulting News*, www.managementconsultingnews.com/interviews/cialdini_interview.php.

Chapter 2

1. Jeffrey Fox interview, "Meet the MasterMinds: Sales Strategies of a Rainmaker with Jeffrey Fox," *Management Consulting News*, www.managementconsultingnews.com/interviews/fox_interview.php.

Chapter 3

1. Socrates quote is from Greek philosopher Diogenes Leartius, *Lives of Eminent Philosophers*, 469 BC–399 BC.
2. *How Clients Buy: 2009 Benchmark Report on Professional Services Marketing and Selling from the Client Perspective*, RainToday.com and Wellesley Hills Group, LLC, 2009, pp. 44–45.

Chapter 4

1. Bertrand Russell quote is from The Quotations Page, www.quotationspage.com/quote/32858.html.

Chapter 6

1. Andy Wood interview, "Meet the MasterMinds: Andy Wood on the Role of Trust in Selling," *Management Consulting News*, www.managementconsult ingnews.com/interviews/wood_interview.php.
2. This list is from the Andy Wood interview in "Meet the MasterMinds," as cited, which was based on the research paper by John Andy Wood, James S. Boles, Wesley Johnston, and Danny Bellenger, "Buyers' Trust of the Salesperson: An Item-Level Meta-Analysis," *Journal of Personal Selling & Sales Management*, vol. XXVIII, no. 3 (summer 2008), pp. 263–283.
3. In the Andy Wood interview in "Meet the MasterMinds," as cited, Professor Wood had this to say about expertise: "The salesperson's expertise is so important that it bypasses trustworthiness and goes straight to trust. Buyers may like you and judge you to be trustworthy, but if you don't know your stuff, they are not going to take the actions that signal trust. To earn trust, you have to show that you have subject-matter expertise and deep product knowledge, and that you are capable, competent, and well-qualified on the matter at hand."

Chapter 7

1. *Selling and Sales Management in the Complex Selling Environment: Executive Summary of Miller Heiman's 2008 Sales Best Practices Study,* Miller Heiman, Inc., 2008, p. 4.

Chapter 8

1. The quote from economist Kenneth Boulding is from Gaia Community, www .gaia.com/quotes/Kenneth_Boulding.
2. Information on Mordecai Brown is from wikipedia.org/wiki/Mordecai_Brown.
3. Information on the physics of curveballs is from http://ffden-2.phys.uaf.edu/ 211_fall2002.web.dir/jon_drobnis/curveball.html.

Chapter 9

1. Mark Stevens, *Your Marketing Sucks* (New York: Crown Business, 2003), p. 50.
2. Figures on revenue from U.S. Census Bureau, North American Industry Classification System (NAICS) report, "Estimated Quarterly Revenue for Employer Firms, First Quarter 2006," for NAICS code 54, Professional, Scientific, and Technical Services.

3. Stephen King, *On Writing: A Memoir of the Craft* (New York: Pocket Books, 2000), p. 124.

Chapter 10

1. Einstein quote is from BrainyQuote, www.brainyquote.com/quotes/quotes/a/ alberteins163057.html.
2. Carmine Gallo, *Inspire Your Audience: 7 Keys to Influential Presentations* (white paper, 2007), p. 3. Gallo refers to the "More than 40 million Power-Point® presentations" people give every day.
3. Judy A. Wagner and Noreen M. Klein, "Who Wants to Go First? Order Effects within a Series of Competitive Sales Presentations," *Journal of Personal Selling & Sales Management*, vol. XXVII, no. 3 (summer 2007), p. 261.
4. Sydney Finkelstein, Jo Whitehead, and Andrew Campbell, *Think Again: Why Good Leaders Make Bad Decisions and How to Keep It from Happening to You* (Boston: Harvard Business Press, 2009), p. 44.
5. Wagner and Klein, "Who Wants to Go First?" as cited, pp. 259–276.

Chapter 12

1. *Selling and Sales Management in the Complex Selling Environment: Executive Summary of Miller Heiman's 2008 Sales Best Practices Study,* Miller Heiman, Inc., 2008, pp. 4–5.

Chapter 13

1. Ford Harding interview, "Meet the Masterminds: Ford Harding on Rainmaking for Consultants," *Management Consulting News*, www.managementconsultingnews.com/interviews/harding_interview2.php.
2. Ford Harding, "Dealing with Unreturned Phone Calls," *Management Consulting News*, www.managementconsultingnews.com/articles/harding_phone_calls.php.

Chapter 15

1. All the statistics in this paragraph are from *Selling and Sales Management in the Complex Selling Environment: Executive Summary of Miller Heiman's 2008 Sales Best Practices Study,* Miller Heiman, Inc., 2008, pp. 7–8.

Client Relationship Development

Capon, Noel. *Key Account Management and Planning: The Comprehensive Handbook for Managing Your Company's Most Import Strategic Asset*. New York: Free Press, 2001.

Dawson, Ross. *Developing Knowledge-Based Client Relationships: The Future of Professional Services*. 2nd ed. Boston: Butterworth-Heinemann, 2005.

Ferrazzi, Keith, and Tahl Raz. *Never Eat Alone: And Other Secrets to Success, One Relationship at a Time*. New York: Doubleday Business, 2005.

Levinson, Jay Conrad, and Michael W. McLaughlin. *Guerrilla Marketing for Consultants: Breakthrough Tactics for Winning Profitable Clients*. Hoboken: John Wiley & Sons, 2005.

Sobel, Andrew. *All for One: 10 Strategies for Building Trusted Client Partnerships*. Hoboken: John Wiley & Sons, 2009.

Toppin, Gilbert, and Fiona Czerniawska. *Business Consulting: A Guide to How it Works and How to Make it Work*. London: The Economist in Association with Profile Books Ltd., 2005.

Communication and Presentation Skills

Atkinson, Cliff. *Beyond Bullet Points: Using Microsoft® Office PowerPoint® 2007 to Create Presentations That Inform, Motivate, and Inspire*. Redmond: Microsoft Press, 2007.

Heath, Chip, and Dan Heath. *Made to Stick: Why Some Ideas Survive and Others Die*. New York: Random House, 2007.

Morgan, Nick. *Trust Me: Four Steps to Authenticity and Charisma*. Hoboken: John Wiley & Sons, 2009.

Patterson, Kerry, Joseph Grenny, David Maxfield, Ron McMillan, and Al Switzler. *Influencer: The Power to Change Anything*. New York: McGraw-Hill, 2007.

Reynolds, Garr. *Presentation Zen: Simple Ideas on Presentation Design and Delivery*. Berkeley: New Riders Press, 2008.

Roam, Dan. *The Back of the Napkin: Solving Problems and Selling Ideas with Pictures*. New York: Portfolio Hardcover, 2008.

Stone, Douglas, Bruce Patton, and Sheila Heen. *Difficult Conversations: How to Discuss What Matters Most*. New York: Penguin Group, 1999.

Weissman, Jerry. *Presenting to Win: The Art of Telling Your Story*. Updated edition. Upper Saddle River: Financial Times Prentice Hall, 2008.

Leadership and Management

Bridges, William. *Managing Transitions: Making the Most of Change*. Cambridge: Perseus Publishing, 2003.

Godin, Seth. *Tribes: We Need You to Lead Us*. New York: Portfolio Hardcover, 2008.

Kouzes, James M., and Barry Z. Posner. *The Leadership Challenge*. 4th ed. San Francisco: Jossey-Bass, 2007.

Kotter, John P. *A Sense of Urgency*. Boston: Harvard Business School Publishing, 2008.

———. *Leading Change*. Boston: Harvard Business School Publishing, 1996.

Lees, Robert J., Thomas J. Delong, and John J. Gabarro. *When Professionals Have to Lead: A New Model for High Performance*. Boston: Harvard Business School Publishing, 1996.

Lencioni, Patrick M. *The Five Dysfunctions of a Team: A Leadership Fable*. San Francisco: Jossey-Bass, 2002.

Prahalad, C. K., and Krishnan, M. S. *The New Age of Innovation: Driving Cocreated Value Through Global Networks*. New York: McGraw-Hill, 2008.

Schaffer, Robert H. *High-Impact Consulting: How Clients and Consultants Can Work Together to Achieve Extraordinary Results*. San Francisco: Jossey-Bass, 2002.

Problem Diagnosis and Solution Development

Buzan, Tony, and Barry Buzan. *The Mind Map Book: How to Use Radiant Thinking to Maximize Your Brain's Untapped Potential*. New York: Penguin Books, 1993.

Finkelstein, Sydney, Jo Whitehead, and Andrew Campbell. *Think Again: Why Good Leaders Make Bad Decisions and How to Keep It from Happening to You*. Boston: Harvard Business School Publishing, 2009.

Gelb, Michael J. *Discover Your Genius: How to Think Like History's Ten Most Revolutionary Minds*. New York: HarperCollins, 2002.

Wind, Yoram (Jerry), and Colin Cook. *The Power of Impossible Thinking: Transform the Business of Your Life and the Life of Your Business*. Upper Saddle River: Wharton School Publishing, 2006.

Sales Proposal Development
and Business Writing

Bacon, Terry R., and David G. Pugh. *Powerful Proposals: How to Give Your Business the Winning Edge*. New York: AMACOM, 2005.

O'Conner, Patricia T. *Words Fail Me: What Everyone Who Writes Should Know About Writing*. New York: Harcourt Brace & Company, 1999.

Sant, Tom. *Persuasive Business Proposals: Writing to Win More Customers, Clients and Contracts*. New York: AMACOM, 2004.

Zinsser, William. *On Writing Well: The Classic Guide to Writing Nonfiction*. New York: HarperCollins, 1976.

Selling and Negotiating

Beckwith, Harry. *What Clients Love: A Field Guide to Growing Your Business*. New York: Warner Books, 2003.

Cialdini, Robert B. *Influence: Science and Practice*. 5th ed. Upper Saddle River: Allyn & Bacon, 2008.

Fox, Jeffrey J. *How to Become a Marketing Superstar: Unexpected Rules That Ring the Cash Register*. New York: Hyperion, 2003.

Harding, Ford. *Rain Making: The Professional's Guide to Attracting New Clients*. 2nd ed. Holbrook: Adams Media Corporation, 2008.

———. *Cross-Selling Success: A Rainmaker's Guide to Professional Account Development*. Holbrook: Adams Media Corporation, 2002.

Konrath, Jill. *Selling to Big Companies*. Chicago: Dearborn Trade Publishing, 2005.

Lax, David A., and James K. Sebenius. *3-D Negotiation: Powerful Tools to Change the Game in Your Most Important Deals*. Boston: Harvard Business School Publishing, 2006.

Thull, Jeff. *Exceptional Selling: How the Best Connect and Win in High Stakes Sales*. Hoboken: John Wiley & Sons, 2006.

Michael W. McLaughlin is the founder and a principal with MindShare Consulting LLC, a firm that creates innovative sales and marketing strategies for professional services companies. He's also the coauthor of *Guerrilla Marketing for Consultants* and the publisher of *Management Consulting News* and *The Guerrilla Consultant,* which reach a global audience of professional service providers. Before founding MindShare Consulting, he was a partner with Deloitte Consulting, where he spent more than two decades working with some of Deloitte's highest-profile clients. You can find out more at www.MindShareConsulting.com and www.ManagementConsultingNews.com.

Also by
Michael W. McLaughlin

Author of the GUERRILLA MARKETING series, with more than one million copies sold

GUERRILLA
MARKETING
FOR
CONSULTANTS

Breakthrough Tactics for
Winning Profitable Clients

JAY CONRAD LEVINSON
MICHAEL W. McLAUGHLIN